MURILLO

ARTBOOKS

FROM CRESCENT MOON PUBLISHING

Leonardo da Vinci
by James Pearson

Early Netherlandish Painting
by Rosalind Mutter

Memling
By W.H.J. & J.C. Weale

Van Eyck
By J. Cyril M. Weale

Piero della Francesca
by Naomi Haskell

Giovanni Bellini
by Julia Davis

Eric Gill: Nuptials of God
by Anthony Hoyland

Minimal Art and Artists In the 1960s and After
by Laura Garrard

Vincent van Gogh: Visionary Landscapes
by Stuart Morris

Mark Rothko: The Art of Transcendence
by Julia Davis

Jasper Johns
by L.M. Poole

Brice Marden
by Laura Garrard

Frank Stella: American Abstract Artist
by James Pearson

Maurice Sendak and the Art of Children's Book Illustration
by L.M. Poole

Sex in Art: Pornography and Pleasure in Painting and Sculpture
by Cassidy Hughes

The Art of Andy Goldsworthy
by William Malpas

Andy Goldsworthy: Touching Nature
by William Malpas

Andy Goldsworthy In Close-Up
by William Malpas

Andy Goldsworthy In America
by William Malpas

Andy Goldsworthy: Pocket Guide
by William Malpas

The Art of Richard Long
by William Malpas

Richard Long: Pocket Guide
by William Malpas

Constantin Brancusi: Sculpting the Essence of Things
by James Pearson

Alison Wilding: The Embrace of Sculpture
by Susan Quinnell

Erotic Art In the 19th Century
By Cassidy Hughes

Erotic Art In the Renaissance
By Cassidy Hughes

Erotic Art
By Cassidy Hughes

The Erotic Object: Sexuality in Sculpture From Prehistory to the Present Day
by Susan Quinnell

Land Art: A Complete Guide
by William Malpas

Land Art In Close-Up
by William Malpas

Land Art In Great Britain
by William Malpas

Land Art In the U.S.A.
by William Malpas

Installation Art In Close-Up
by William Malpas

Colorfield Painting
by Laura Garrard

Bellini
By James Mason

Botticelli
By Henry Binns

Renaissance In Italy: The Fine Arts
By John Addington Symonds

The Life of Michelangelo Buonarroti
By John Addington Symonds

Michelangelo Buonarroti
By Charles Holroyd

Michelangelo
By Estelle Hurll

Michelangelo
By Romain Rolland

Correggio
By Estelle M. Hurll

Tintoretto
By S.L. Bensusan

Titian: A Collection of Fifteen Pictures
By Estelle M. Hurll

The Earlier Work of Titian
By Claude Phillips

The Later Work of Titian
By Claude Phillips

The Earlier and Later Work of Titian
By Claude Phillips

Bernardino Luini
By James Mason

Perugino
By Selwyn Brinton

Perugino
By George Williamson

Raphael
By Estelle M. Hurll

Raphael
By Paul Konody

Dante Gabriel Rossetti
By Esther Wood

Recollections of Dante Gabriel Rossetti
By T. Hall Caine

Burne-Jones
By A. Lys Baldry

The Whistler Book
By Sadakichi Hartmann

Whistler
By T. Martin Wood

Rodin: The Man and His Art
Edited by Judith Cladel

Rodin
By Rainer Maria Rilke

Auguste Rodin
By Camille Mauclair

Corot
By Sidney Allnutt

Fra Angelico
By Jennie Ellis Keysor

Fra Angelico
By James Mason

Fra Angelico
By J.B. Supino

Aubrey Beardsley
By Robert Ross

The Art of Aubrey Beardsley
By Arthur Symons

Leighton
By Ernest Rhys

Millais
By A. Lys Baldry

The Madonna In Art
By Estelle Hurll

Women In the Fine Arts
By Clara Erskine Clement

The Venetian School of Painting
By Evelyn Phillipps

Boucher
By Haldane McFall

Fragonard
By Haldane McFall

Leonardo da Vinci
By Maurice Brockwell

Famous European Painters
By Sarah Bolton

Great Artists
By Jennie Ellis Keysor

Great Pictures
Edited by Esther Singleton

Knights of Art
By Amy Steedman

Delacroix
By Paul Konody

Ingres
By A.J. Finberg

Goya
By Francis Crastre

Dürer
By Hertbert Furst

Albrecht Dürer
By T. Sturge Moore

Dürer
By M.F. Sweetser

Rembrandt van Rijn
By Malcolm Bell

Rembrandt and His Works
By John Burnet

Rembrandt and His Etchings
By Louis Holman

Rembrandt
By Estelle M. Hurll

Rembrandt
By Josef Israels

Turner
By C. Lewis Hind

Turner
By W. Cosmo Monkhouse

The Art of Katsuhiro Otomo
By Jeremy Robinson

The Art of Masamune Shirow
By Jeremy Robinson

MURILLO

S.L. BENSUSAN

CRESCENT MOON

First published 1910. This edition © 2021. Reprint 2023.

Set in Book Antiqua 10 on 14pt.
Designed by Radiance Graphics.

Thanks to the authors and publishers quoted.

British Library Cataloguing in Publication data

ISBN-13 9781861716354
ISBN-13 9781861718938

CRESCENT MOON PUBLISHING
P.O. Box 1312, Maidstone, Kent, ME14 5XU
Great Britain, www.crmoon.com

CONTENTS

NOTE ON THE TEXT

The text is from *Murillo* by S.L. Bensusan, and published by T.C. & E.C. Jack, London, 1910.

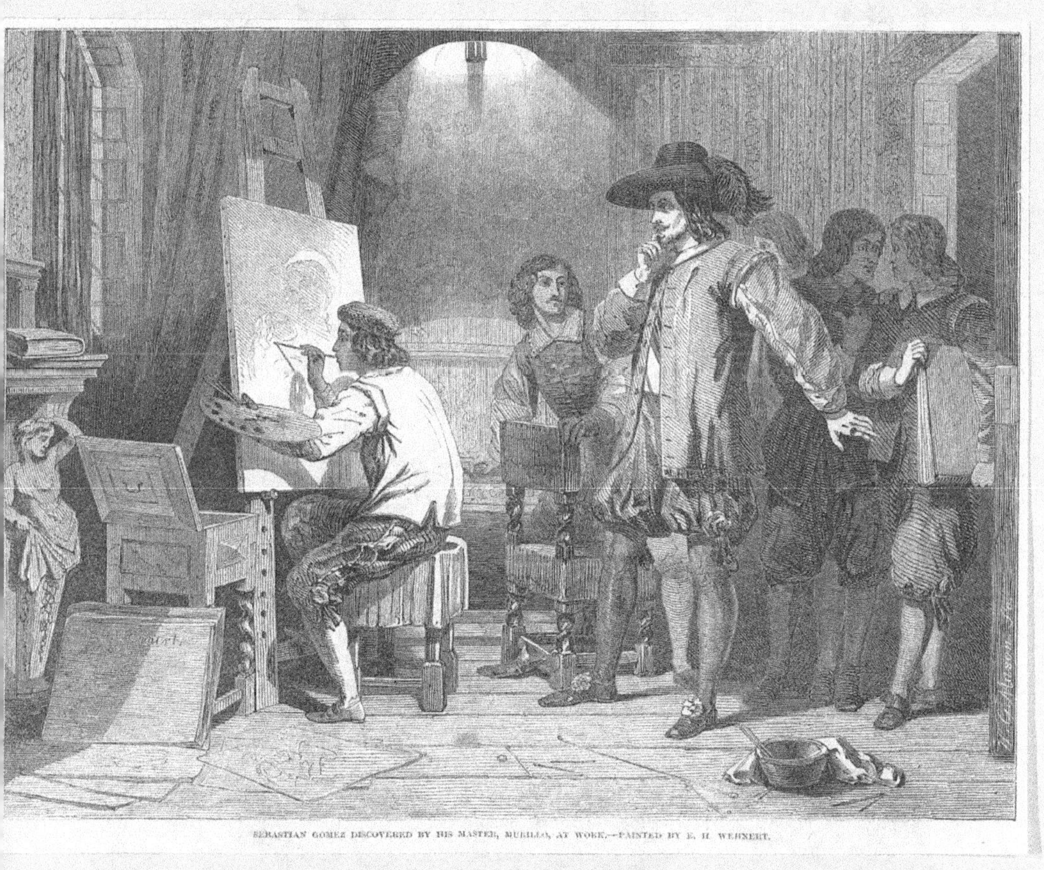

SEBASTIAN GOMEZ DISCOVERED BY HIS MASTER, MURILLO, AT WORK.—PAINTED BY E. H. WEHNERT.

Sebastian Gomez Discovere By His Master Murillo, At Work
from the "Illustrated London News", 1848

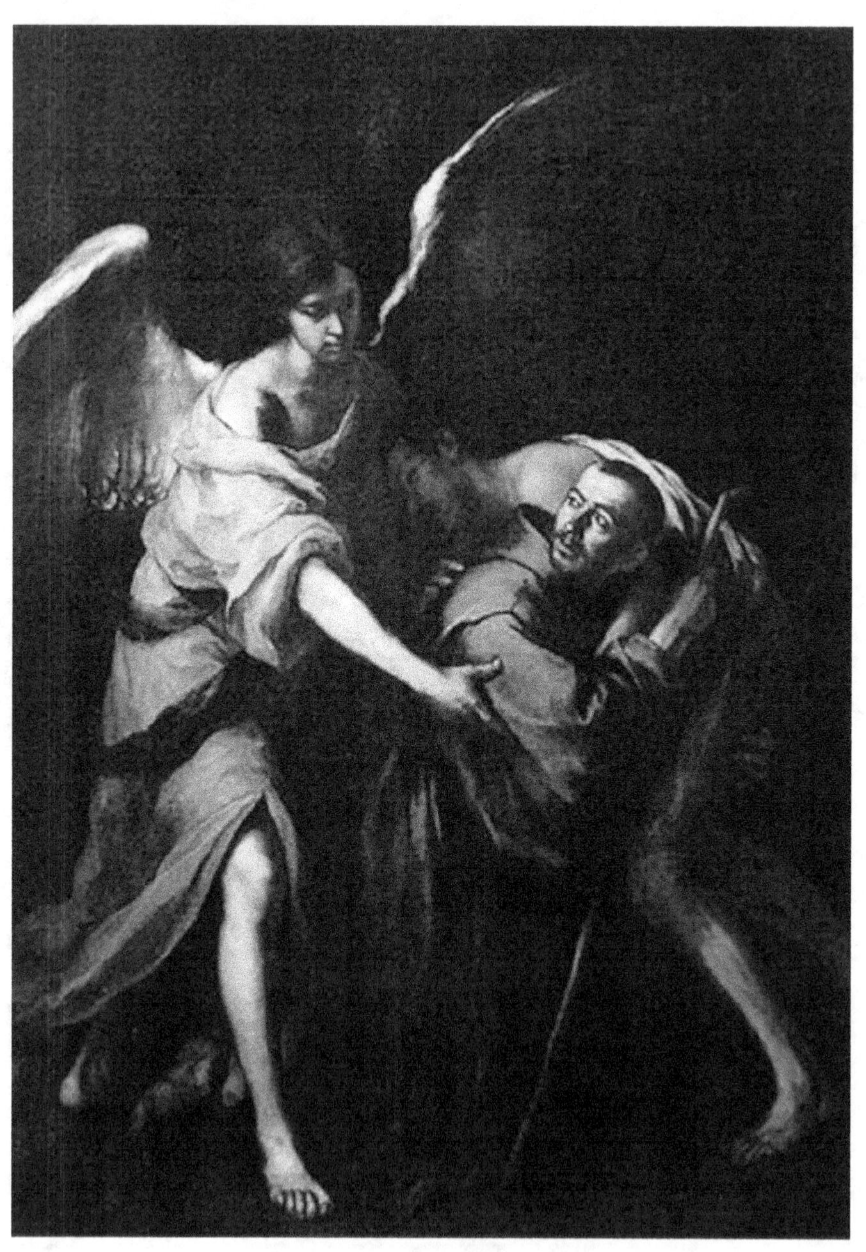

B.E. Murillo, John of God, 1665-72

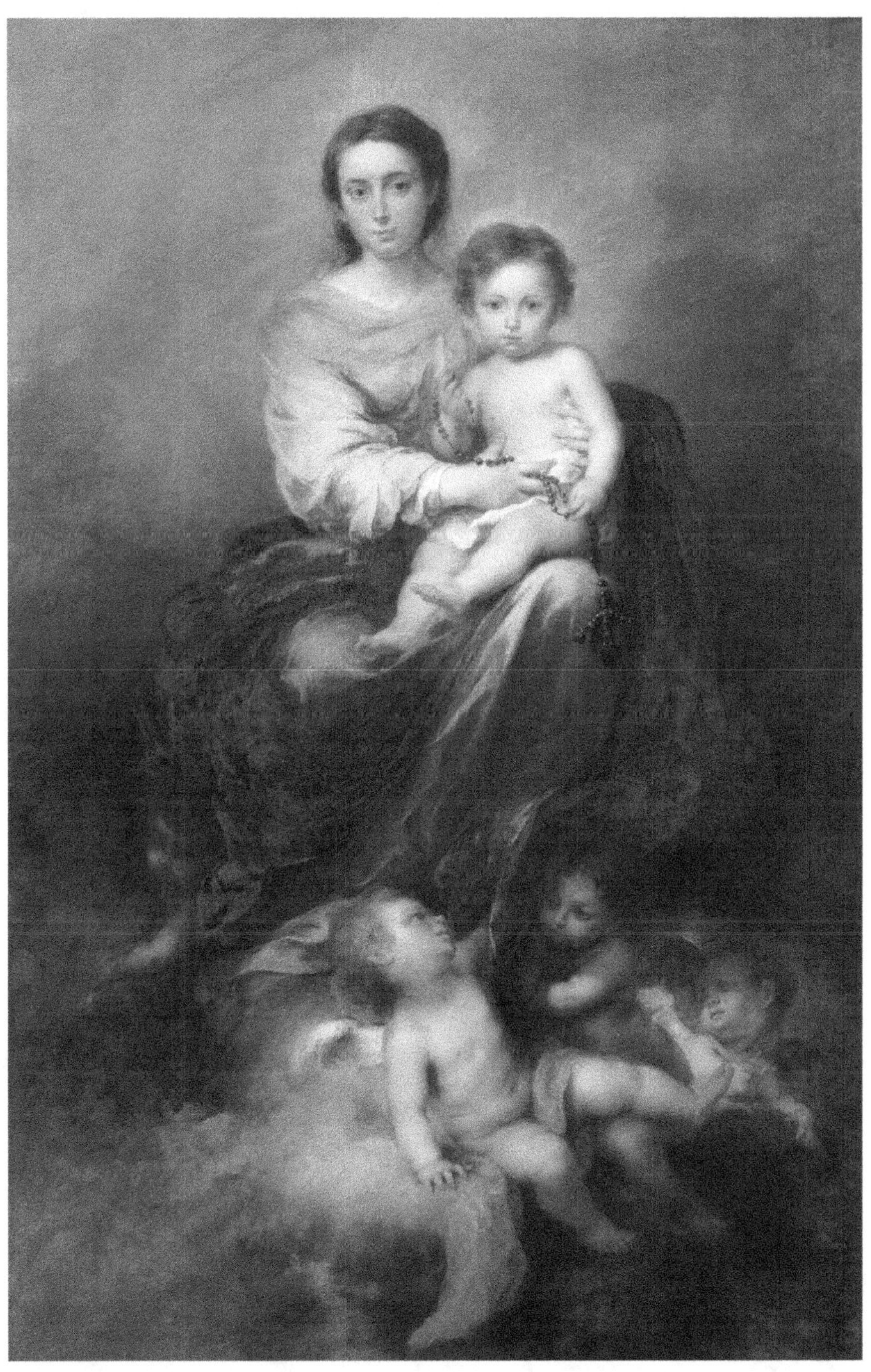

B.E. Murillo, The Madonna of the Rosary,
1675-80, Dulwich, London

I

There have been long years in which the name of Bartolomé Esteban, known to the world as Murillo, was one to conjure with. Velazquez, El Greco, Ribera, Zurburan, Goya, were long uncertain in their appeal, recognised only by the enlightened among their contemporaries and ignored by the great majority of their fellow-countrymen. The pendulum of taste swings slowly from one extreme to the other, and, as the moods and needs of men change so they cast their idols into the dust, where they remain until another generation restores what it can find to the old pedestals. Nowadays Murillo has fallen from his high estate among the elect; they prefer to magnify his shortcomings rather than to acknowledge his many merits, to ignore the splendid service he rendered to Spanish art and the profound effect of his pictures in drawing countless simple souls within the sheltering folds of the Church. The fifty years of his devoted labours count for nothing, the self-searching and criticism that enabled the painter to move from a low plane to a high one are forgotten. This is not as it should be. Bartolomé Esteban Murillo had his limitations, but remains, despite them all, one of the world's teachers, and such glimpses of his life as may be seen through the shadows of some two hundred and fifty years reveal him as a serious artist who added to splendid natural gifts a steadfastness of purpose, a determination to do his best, a love of Andalusia, and a devotion to the religion in which he was brought up that must compel the admiration of thinking men however critical, and enable the artist to stand alone. In the early years of his sojourn he suffered from the pinch of poverty. He was born when Diego de Silva Velazquez was just about to enter upon his splendid career, in fact, Murillo would have been about five years old when his great contemporary left Seville for Madrid. Perhaps if we could see with understanding eyes we might be tempted to believe that the less distinguished artist enjoyed the happier life, for Velazquez in the court of kings had much to endure that never troubled the younger man who laboured in the service of the King of kings, and may have seen such visions as lightened the labours of Beato Angelico in the Convent of the Dominicans of St. Anthony in Padua, and St. Francis in Assisi. For the best of Murillo's canvases whisper to us of inspiration, of devout belief, and of an overmastering love for the "Maria santissima," and when the simple-hearted painter saw that his work brought honour to the cathedrals and convents for which he laboured he must have felt that his art was its own exceeding great reward.

To this day Andalusia is a country of dreamers, and Seville, despite its electric trams and motor cars, its barracks and cosmopolitan hostelries, is *par excellence* the city of dreams. How much more so then, three hundred years ago, when Murillo was born to enjoy its beauty? In Seville wealth is a mere accident, even the poor may return thanks without mental reservation for the nugatory gift of life. Faith flourishes to-day in the agnostic generation as of old time, blended with what we would regard as superstition, but sharing this fault with all the Latin countries. In the Cathedral and the Caridad, to say nothing of smaller religious houses, the pictures of Murillo still remind us that to the Catholic religion the world owes the worship of a woman. To Murillo, God and the Virgin were not pale abstractions; they were his father and his mother, for he was hardly more than ten years old when his earthly parents fell victims to one of the epidemics so common in Europe in days when sanitation and isolation were not understood.

For twenty years, the most impressionable of his life, Murillo lived alone. Those who sneer at his work in these early times ignore the conditions under which it was done, forget that the cost of canvas and pigment was a very serious item in his exchequer, and that his reward was of the smallest. Wealth never came his way until he was no longer quite young, but as his circumstances became easier he did all that in him lay to express his message more completely and, while his labour was unremitting, his last work was his best, and included masterpieces that may hold their own in any company, even though it include the masters before whom artist and layman bow the head. Murillo has been cheapened by forgers and copyists who have succeeded in placing many of his shortcomings and very little of his quality on their hurried canvases. Every picture dealer in a Spanish city of any pretensions has a Murillo or two that he is prepared to vouch for even though the canvas gives the lie to his protestations. The artist's work has been used shamelessly for purposes of advertisement, it has paid the fullest penalties of popularity, and yet, a real Murillo in the best manner is a picture to which we can turn again and again, to find over and above the conquest of technical difficulties and the beauties of colour the qualities of imagination and inspiration that are associated with the select few in every branch of creative work. One might go as far as to say that Seville would lose as much as Madrid if the Murillos were taken from the one and the Velazquez pictures from the other. There would be no hesitation on the writer's part to say as much if the capital of Andalusia had never been rifled of its proper store by the French conquerors of Spain. It is not in foreign galleries that one must go to see the work of a great artist, but in the city that was his home – the city wherein the sources of his inspiration linger and his pictures find an appropriate setting. Transplanting is not good for anything. The trees and flowers, the birds and beasts of a foreign land may endure in a clime for which they were not intended, but there is no more than an arrested growth; they cannot do justice to themselves. Frankly and without reserve we admit that Murillo was almost as much an Andalusian as a painter, but when we know his city and his work there, a fine picture in the National Gallery or the Louvre will bring Seville back to us as surely as a sea-shell brings back the ceaseless murmur of the waves.

II

THE ARTIST'S LIFE

Murillo came into the world with the close of the year 1617, and was baptized in a church destroyed during the French invasion nearly two hundred years later; the record of his baptism is preserved to-day in the Church of St. Paul. History is silent about his early years, but the authorities make it clear that his parents were among the very poorest of the city and that he was brought up in the old Jewish quarter, always the abiding place of indigence and suffering. In all probability he roamed the streets of the Triana and the Arrebola, little better off than the beggar boys who were destined to provide so much striking material for his brush. When his parents died of the plague that visited Seville the lad and his sister were adopted by an uncle who was a struggling doctor. Times were bad in spite of the epidemic; probably there was more demand than payment for medical services of the quality that Don Juan Lagares could offer: but his little nephew's cleverness with brush and pencil was too obvious to escape notice, and Don Juan del Castillo, one of the city's leading painters, was induced by the doctor to accept the lad as a pupil without payment of a fee.

In the studio of a moderately successful artist a pupil would be required to do menial work – to grind colours, clean brushes, sweep floors; he would pick up what he could of the master's methods when he had nothing else to do. It was no good apprenticeship for a beginner whose youthful talent required direction from a bigger man, but beggars cannot be choosers, and doubtless uncle and nephew were grateful to Castillo, who has few claims upon our memory save in his capacity as master of Seville's great painter. He found a willing pupil whose work was admitted to some of the poorer religious houses in the city when he was only fifteen, and the relations between the two would seem to have been pleasant, for Murillo worked in the studio for ten years or more, and probably received some small regular payment in return for his services as soon as he had demonstrated their value. Then Juan del Castillo moved to Cadiz, and Murillo remained in Seville. Judging by his actions in years to come, he remained because the city was very dear to him; he would undoubtedly have been useful to his master, and beyond doubt the closing of Castillo's workshop left him at the age of twenty-three in dire financial straits. He had his sister to support, and the means of doing so were of the smallest, for he was only known to the poorer brethren of the Church who had few commissions to offer and very little to pay for them. The best paid work was in strong hands and, if no high dignitaries of the Church in Seville knew much about the struggling painter, it must be confessed that he had not done much to attract or to deserve attention. He was an artist in the making just then, and the making was a slow and painful process.

Without the means for pursuit of serious study and with urgent need for present pence, the young painter was forced to do as the lowest members of his class were doing, and he did work not unlike that with which needy gentlemen adorn street corners in our own year of grace. To be sure he did not choose a pitch and decorate it with busts of the reigning family, the ruling minister, a church, a ship at anchor, and a flock of sheep in a snowstorm, but he purchased the cheapest and coarsest cloth he could buy, cut it up, stretched it, and painted pictures for the Fair.

At least once a week there would be a Fair in the Triana or Macarena, every day would witness the arrival there of country farmers and dealers with something to buy or sell; and when a man's store or purse was full, when he had eaten well, and was conscious of the joy of life, he would often consent to become a patron of the arts in response to the petition of some needy son of the brush who showed him a flaming, flaring picture of a Madonna or a Holy Family, or produced a piece of unspoilt saga-cloth and offered to paint a portrait almost as quickly as the itinerant photographer of Brighton beach or Margate sands can prepare the counterfeit of his victim with the aid of evil-smelling collodion plates. Such pictures were always to be bought at the Feria, though the writer has not found itinerant artists at the Fairs of either Seville or Cordova in the past few years – perhaps they can make more money by painting "genuine Murillos" for small dealers and owners of shops that sell second-hand goods. Doubtless, the young painter was a quick worker, his gifts in those days were readily expressed, and when he lacked a commission from any of the visitors to the Fair he prepared a few canvases for traders who sent them to the religious houses of South America, where the influence of Spain was so widely and heavily felt. It is not easy to guess how long he would have been content with such work, but when he had followed it for about two years a great change came into his life, and for the first time he became acquainted with better things.

In the studio or workshop of Juan del Castillo he had formed a friendship with a lad from Granada, one Pedro Moya, who, on leaving Castillo, seems to have followed art and war and to have served his native land in the Low Countries, where there were ample chances for the soldier of fortune who had the good luck to pass unscathed across the stricken field. Moya's talent was stimulated by a chance acquaintance with Van Dyck's work, and in order to study this great master he retired from the army and left for London, where Van Dyck, then in the last year of his life, admitted him as a pupil. When Van Dyck had passed away, Moya found his occupation gone, so he left our fogbound shores for his native Andalusia, took up his residence in Seville, and renewed his friendship with his old friend and fellow-student. Murillo soon found in his friend's work qualities he had never seen before; they revealed the poverty of his own efforts, and filled him with an overmastering desire to travel and to learn. It was easier to feel the desire than to respond to it. Italy, then as now the Mecca of the Spanish artist, was far beyond his reach, but he had heard stories of the success that had come to his fellow-countryman Velazquez in Madrid, and thought that if he could go to him he would gain a little of the advice and instruction of which he stood so much in need. With this idea he entered into an arrangement with a picture exporter, who carried on a large trade with South America, and undertook to paint a large number of works at a special price. Working at high pressure he completed the order, received his pay, placed his young sister under the care of friends, and shook the dust of the Macarena from his feet. His road lay towards the North, and once in the capital of Spain, he presented himself before Velazquez.

We do not know much about the private life and character of the greatest of Spanish painters, but the little that is known is all to his credit. He did not hesitate to take the raw, ill-trained lad of five-and-twenty under his protection, though his only claims upon the Court painter were his talent and such kinship as may be said to exist between two men, the one distinguished, the other unknown, who hail from the same city. What Velazquez did was done thoroughly. As soon as he was satisfied of the *bonâ fides* of his visitor, he gave him a home, examined his work, and pointed out its defects, procured his admission to the royal galleries, and advised him to copy the work of Ribera and Van Dyck. These opportunities were all Murillo required. He could not have seen or hoped to see Velazquez very often, for the Court painter was a man whose leisure was much restricted, but he settled down to his work, and for two years or more was a painstaking copyist who lacked no opportunities. Velazquez, not content to do all he could unaided, had even shown his pupil's work to his own patron the Duke of Olivares then still at the zenith of his power and, either directly or through Olivares, had brought it before the notice of the king. When Velazquez returned from Lerida in 1644, Murillo had made so much progress that his patron thought he was quite fit to complete his studies in Italy, and offered him the necessary introductions and money.

All lovers of Murillo must wish that he had availed himself of the opportunity, but in the circumstances it is not altogether surprising that he did not. Doubtless, he had heard Seville calling through all the days and nights of his sojourn in Castile. Madrid is not a pleasant city to those who know the South, and then, too, the young painter would have been lonely, and must have remembered that his sister, his only near relative, would be anxiously awaiting his return. He had learned a great deal; he may have felt that his gifts such as they were would secure him a good living in his own city, perhaps he felt he had assimilated as much as he could express for many years to come. We cannot tell what was in his mind, though to those of us who have fallen under the spell of Seville there is not much difficulty in forming an opinion about it, and we are inclined to think that his decision offended his splendid patron, for the two great Sevillians never met again. Henceforward Murillo's home was to be in the city of his birth, and his work was to be limited by the commissions that the city could yield him. Doubtless, he travelled gladly to the South to take up his residence in the Plaza de Alfaro, and display his latest work to men who might possibly become his patrons. He had left Seville unknown and undistinguished, now he had enjoyed the advantage of training under the greatest Sevillian of all.

He was still poor, and his poverty induced him to accept an ill-paid commission from the fathers of the Franciscan convent for eleven pictures. Fresh from the long course of study in Madrid, conscious that this his first chance might be his last if he did not do his best, he set to work and produced a series that roused the city to enthusiasm. Literally, he woke one morning to find himself famous. The Franciscan convent was destroyed by fire in 1810, but the pictures were not lost, for Marshal Soult had carried off ten out of eleven, and the other had passed into the gallery of a Spanish grandee on its way to this country. The French invaders of Spain were connoisseurs as well as soldiers, and in consideration of their *flair* we may at this time of day overlook the shortcomings in their ethical code. Murillo had made the Franciscan convent famous; the Franciscans had put their painter beyond the reach of monetary trouble and had settled for him the lines his talent was to follow. The painter of a picture, like the writer of a book or a play, must pay this one tribute to success; he must do the work that the public looks for. Should he venture to discover himself in other directions his early patrons will turn and rend him. Happily the whole trend of this artistic talent was in the direction of sacred picture painting, and in the years that follow we find little else from his hand save a few portraits and a landscape or two of minor importance.

It may occur to the reader to ask what was the special quality of Murillo's work that made so prompt an appeal to his countrymen, and the answer is not far to seek. Hitherto sacred subjects had been dealt with in most unattractive fashion. Art, the handmaiden of the Church, had delighted in the presentation of ascetic figures as far removed from struggling humanity as the heavens are above the earth. Saints and martyrs looking as though they were newly escaped from the grip of the Inquisition were to be met with on every side; the virtues, the kindliness, and even the humanity of the lives of saints and devotees altogether were ignored. Murillo peopled his canvas with an entirely new class of people, as human and as fascinating as the Sevillians themselves. On Murillo's canvases his fellow-countrymen saw no more long-drawn agonies of martyrdom, but gracious Madonnas and delightful Children, and Saints who had not been soured in the pursuit of righteousness. It was a revelation to Andalusia this strange new view of holiness, this mingling of the heavens with the earth, this insistence upon a common bond that united the aureoled saint with the sick beggar to whom he gave alms. Then, too, the rich almost sensuous colouring of the new work was a quality hitherto unknown to Seville, although we may wonder why some of the Spaniards from other cities, who may have been warm colourists, had not been attracted to sun-loving Seville, where they could have created an immediate market for work that responded to the unvarying humour of the people.

The painter's studio was now thronged with the *élite* of Seville, by the crowds that muster when genius has been acclaimed by responsible parties and they need have no fear of their own taste. The man who had painted *pinturas de la feria* only three years ago could now choose his own commissions. He made the best use of his opportunities, and, a couple of years after his work for the Franciscans had given him a start in life, he married Dona Beatrice de Cabrera y Sotomayor. A portrait by Murillo said to be of the lady, is in the collection of Sir J. Stirling-Maxwell, but, seen through the medium of a photograph, it does nothing to explain why the painter married her. Perhaps the facts that she was of noble family, and had wealth, may be trusted to provide the key. Her flatterers could hardly have said that she was attractive. In the picture she wears a mantilla, and a flower in her hair after the fashion of the Sevillana, and looks as though she seldom suffered from good temper, but if the portrait does stand for the painter's wife, it is only fair to add that we have no record to suggest that she was as difficult as she appears here. The suggestion that one of his later portraits of a really attractive woman represents his mistress is not supported sufficiently to convince us.

Down to the year of his return to Seville the painter's work is of small importance, and in all probability the most of it has been lost. In a country where the wealthy were better prepared to buy pictures than to attach any importance to those who painted them, it is hardly likely that the rough immature efforts of the painter who sought his patrons at the weekly Fair would command attention. Critics of Murillo divide his works into three periods, the first dating from 1646 to 1652, when his outlines were hard and the background lacked depth, and the colouring was more or less metallic. Following this came a short period of transition lasting till 1656, when more of the individuality behind the brush becomes expressed on the canvas, and one does not see the joints in the composition, or the definite effects by which the colour scheme has been secured. From 1656 Murillo may be said to have entered into his kingdom, to have expressed his conception of Holy Family and saints as they occurred to his mind, to stand outside the conventions that had fettered him hitherto. Some hold that these changes were merely the result of constant study, but the writer inclines to a strong belief that they were more than the fruit of mere technical efficiency. The painter was turning more and more from things of earth, to what he held to be things of Heaven, his emotional nature was responsive to the ceremonial of the Church, and to the lives of its worthiest representatives. Nearly all his work was done, whether directly or indirectly, in the service of the Faith, and he learned devoutly to believe in the miracles he was asked to express on canvas. Then it was that he sought to represent female forms of simple but enduring beauty, making luminous the surrounding air, angels hovering over saints, little cherubs, whose feet had never touched our own hard earth, smiling from folds of the Madonna's robes.

Unconsciously, perhaps, he was doing as the Florentine and Venetian painters of the Renaissance had done before him; he was studying the motherhood and childhood in the streets around him, and transferring it with sure touch and reverent hand to his canvas. Small wonder then that his work in the latter days went home more directly than ever to the people among whom he lived, and that they looked upon Murillo as they looked upon the Cathedral, or the Giralda Tower, as a monument to their city and an instruction to strangers. To this day in the ancient city if you would praise a work of art of any description, you say it is a Murillo, *i.e.* a masterpiece. Perhaps the source of the painter's struggle gives us also the key-note to his weakness. The Church gave him faith and commissions, but it also imposed upon him a certain stilted handling of his subjects. His angels and cherubs came from the streets around his home, and sometimes one feels that they are a little tired, a little intolerant of the pose he has inflicted upon them, and are anxious to return to less unnatural surroundings. For all his facility he had no daring; he felt and uttered the restrictions that the Church imposed. Do not let us blame him for this, we should rather remember his achievement in humanising the heavenly host than his failure to make it human without self-consciousness. Only a wider training and a deeper knowledge in many directions could have freed his brush, but had it been too free, he would have found his occupation gone. There must have been zealous churchmen who looked askance at many of his pictures, for the bulk of these clerics could hardly have looked at art save through the narrowing glasses of theology. To estimate the debt that Spanish art owes to Murillo, let us look at the representation of the subjects he made his own by any of the men who preceded him.

Although Murillo was so largely concerned with sacred art and religious feeling that his pictures for religious houses are largely in excess of all others, he took an intelligent interest in the social and artistic life around him. His home became one of the centres of intellectual communion in a city that has never devoted itself altogether to affairs of the mind, and he associated with the heads of Sevillian society in and out of the Church. The old lean years were far behind him, his pictures commanded the highest prices in the city, and were in demand beyond its boundaries, though it is extremely unlikely that he left Seville for long at any time. He may have gone as far as Cadiz, before he went to his death there, but that would have been the extreme limit of his excursions. Now and again by way of relaxation he painted a landscape – there are one or two in Madrid which have not yet been explained away by critics – and he painted portraits from time to time, though he preferred to give to some saint the features he was asked to record. Doubtless he felt that the Church had the first and final claims upon his services, and that he had no right to devote his time to secular subjects.

As his social influence and his opportunity for intercourse with leading contemporaries increased, he entertained the idea of establishing in Seville a Public Academy of Art. In pursuit of this idea he would have received the hearty encouragement of the ecclesiasts who looked upon art as a sure aid to devotion, and it may be that their assistance contributed largely to the success of the inaugural meeting held in Seville in the beginning of the year 1660, when a score or more of the leading painters of Andalusia drew up the constitution of the new body, and elected Murillo and the younger Herrera as joint Presidents. Students were to be admitted on payment of what they could afford, and the suggestion that the Church was supporting the new venture is justified by the fact that every student was required to abjure profanity and profess his orthodoxy by reciting an established formula. The Presidents devoted a week in turn to the Academy, teaching, criticising, and advising, and the struggling young artists of the city and its environs made haste to avail themselves of the chance of securing tuition and assistance. Herrera did not remain constant to his self-imposed task, and doubtless Murillo found it irksome, but the Academy was to no small extent the creation of his own brain, and he did his best for it, taking up the burden that his fellow president had laid aside. It is clear that he must have possessed some talent for organisation and administration; the Academy seems to have thrived as long as he was able to direct its affairs, but shortly after his death its doors were closed. Some of the Spanish writers who have had access to old papers and correspondence declare that Murillo's position was one of great difficulty from the first, that the jealousy of men who were older and less successful than he hampered him very considerably, and that many of his best intentioned efforts were thwarted. It is not difficult to understand that the painter's extraordinary career had provided him with plenty of detractors, and that his position at the head of the Academy would be resented by the elderly unsuccessful gentlemen who knew that the experiment was being watched from the highest quarters in Madrid.

It is not possible in this place to refer at any length to the important work executed by Murillo in the first fifteen years of his latest manner. To attempt such a task would be to compile a catalogue that could hardly be of interest, save to the few English lovers of Murillo, who know his work in National Gallery, Louvre, Prado, Hermitage, and the public and private collections in Seville. Let it suffice for the moment to point out that he had been honoured with commissions to paint pictures for the Cathedral of Seville, once a Temple to Venus, and possessing to this day, if the writer has been truly informed, dungeons wherein the officers of Holy Inquisition wrought their will upon the *corpus vile* of the heretic. He decorated the Chapel Royal in honour of the canonisation of St. Ferdinand. In the Chapter Room of the Cathedral are eight portraits painted in oval for the dome. All are saints, six men and two women, the latter being St. Justa and St. Rufina, the patron saints of the city. In years to come Goya was asked to paint St. Justa and St. Rufina, and showed his respect for their sanctity by employing two courtesans to sit for the portraits; but this is another story, and belongs to the time of the French war and Ferdinand the Desired. There are countless studies of Christ in the Cathedral, one as a lad, another at the Baptism by St. John, a third in which the child Christ appears to St. Anthony of Padua, another after the scourging. The picture of Christ and St. Anthony was probably one of the finest of the master's works, but it has been vilely restored. As a rule, the gentlemen employed in

Spain to restore masterpieces seem to have as much knowledge of art as the African witch doctor has of the healing art that is practised by a London Doctor of Medicine. It is only now and again, when one finds Murillo at his best in a picture that has defied the assaults of time, that one can realise what the cruel mercies of the restorer have done to obscure the painter's work. They have accentuated the obvious, turned sentiment into sentimentality, and made colour schemes lose their refinement. If Shakespeare's sonnets had been found mutilated, and had been restored by that "philosopher true," the late Martin Tupper, we should have had in literature a counterpart of the result we have here in art.

Beyond Murillo's highly important work in Seville Cathedral, attention must be called to the pictures he painted for the Church of Santa Maria la Blanca, the Convent of the Capuchins, and the Caridad. Only one of them, a "Last Supper," not in the painter's best manner, remains there to-day; but the splendid semicircular picture of the Conception, now in the Louvre, was painted for Santa Maria la Blanca, and hung there until Marshal Soult cast his rapacious, but well cultivated, regard upon it; and in the Academy of San Fernando in Madrid, where so many of the fine Goyas are preserved, we can see two others, "The Dream" and "The Senator and his Wife before the Pope." The story set out is founded upon the legend of a Roman Senator and his wife, who being childless vowed to leave their wealth to the Virgin. She appeared to them in a dream, the infant Christ in her arms, and bade them erect to her a church on the Esquiline, at a spot she indicated. To this dream the Church of Santa Maria Maggiore in Rome is said to owe its foundation. The two canvases stolen or annexed by Soult were returned to Spain after his death.

The Caridad, a well-managed hospital, scrupulously clean, light and airy, thrives to-day on the banks of the Guadalquivir, close to the Tower of the Gold, and doubtless the writer is but one of many who have spent long hours there, content to endure the sights and sounds of suffering for the sake of the remnant of work that still graces the wall of church and hospital. There would be much more than can be seen to-day but for the visits of the indefatigable Marshal Soult, who had such a penchant for the master's work that neither Cathedral nor hospital could guard it from his eyes and hands. It is easy enough to study Murillo in the public galleries, but it seems more satisfactory to see his canvases in the places for which they were painted, and a special interest attaches to the hospital of the Caridad, because it was founded by one of the men whom an age of devout belief is apt to produce from time to time – a desperate sinner turned saint. Don Miguel Manara of Calatrava, born a few years after Murillo, was a man of pleasure who wasted his substance in riotous living. One night as he was reeling home from a debauch he saw a funeral procession approaching him, the open bier surrounded by torch-bearing priests. "Whom do you carry to the grave?" he cried, and one of the priests replied, "Don Miguel Manara." Greatly terrified, the profligate looked at the corpse and recognised the features as his own. Then he knew no more until morning broke and he found himself in a church. Had he lived in this prosaic age his friends would have taken him to a nursing home to enjoy the benefits of bromide and a rest cure, but two hundred and fifty years ago a man had to work out his own salvation. He did so very thoroughly, turned from a profligate to a devotee and, after infinite labour, founded the hospital and church of the Caridad on the ruins of an early building of the same character. It is a splendid institution, and preserves to this day the character proposed by its founder, whose anxious careworn face looks at us from the canvas painted by Juan de Valdes in the Cabilda. Murillo painted ten or eleven pictures for the Church of San Jorge attached to the hospital; three remain: one is in Madrid, and two are in the town house of the Duke of Sutherland. Perhaps the "Moses" is the best of those that remain, but the Saint Elizabeth of Hungary, now in Madrid, is a master work.

Gratitude for such favours as he had received would appear to have been one of the painter's characteristics, and may be held accountable for the splendid effort on behalf of the Franciscans, who in early days had given the commission that made him famous. When the brethren appealed to him in 1673 he was a rich man, and able to work as cheaply as in the days when every real was worth saving. The Convent, then on the outskirts of the city, had taken forty years or more in the building. Now it needed decoration, and the brethren did not appeal in vain to the greatest ecclesiastical painter of the day. We do not know his fee, but we do know that he devoted six years to his task. Upwards of a score of pictures testified at once to his devotion and to his skill, for they are among the best he has painted, and happily the most of them are to be seen in the Murillo Salon of the Seville Museum. The brethren of St. Francis, though they made one or two exchanges of the kind that Glaucus made with Diomedes, had the sense to put the canvases they elected to preserve beyond the reach of Marshal Soult, and the Salon of Trabella holds *inter alia* the "St. Francis at the foot of the Cross," "Justa and Rufina," "St. Thomas of Villanueva," and two Conceptions. It will be remembered that the Papal Edict declaring the Immaculacy of the Mother of God was issued in the year of Murillo's birth, and doubtless many a devout Catholic believed that the painter was given to Spain as a reward to Philip IV. by whose strenuous endeavour Pope Paul V. had issued his momentous decree.

The pictures painted for the Franciscans were held by Murillo's contemporaries to place a crown upon his achievements. Brilliant as his work had been for the Cathedral and the Caridad, for the hospital known as Los Venerables, and for the Church of the Augustines, the Franciscans were held to have been the most fortunate of all the painter's patrons, and his pictures gave an immense stimulus to the labours of the Church. The Capuchins of Cadiz besought him to journey to their city and to paint some pictures for their house. He had already reached a great age and an assured position, and no pecuniary recompense that the Capuchin Friars had to offer could have drawn him from his beloved native city; but the temptation to work for the greater glory of God was irresistible, and he set out. It was an unfortunate journey. While engaged on a picture of the marriage of Santa Catherine, he stumbled in mounting the scaffolding, and ruptured himself badly. Suffering great pain, and unable or unwilling to describe his condition precisely, he was brought back to Seville, and we may feel assured that the journey must have aggravated his symptoms. His children and friends did all they could to alleviate his sufferings, but in those days of elemental knowledge rupture was not readily diagnosed, nor was there any effective treatment. We are told that the dying man was taken every day to the Church of the Holy Cross, where he prayed beneath the shadow of Campana's "Descent." Feeling that his end was upon him he sent for all his family and friends, and with the evening of April 3, 1682, the end came. He was buried under Campana's "Descent from the Cross," and his funeral afforded an occasion for all classes of Seville to show how greatly they respected the distinguished dead. He left but little money, though he had some real estate and a valuable collection of plate and pictures. By his will he left instructions that four hundred masses were to be said for the repose of his soul – a generous allowance surely for one whose life was singularly free from blame. His wife had predeceased him, but his sister, for whom he had laboured in the far-off early days, survived; she had married a distinguished man of noble birth. His children were two sons and a daughter; the elder son was in the West Indies: the second, who took to art, died before middle age.

You may find his work in all the great galleries to-day, but to know Murillo intimately one must go to Spain – to Seville and Madrid for choice. France boasts a fine collection, and many of those that adorn our National Gallery, Dulwich and Wallace Collections, are worthy of the painter. In Rome, Florence, Dresden, Munich, Berlin, Vienna, and St. Petersburg he is represented by work that demands attention. Doubtless much of his output has been lost, much has been restored to death, some pictures remain to be discovered, but it should not be difficult to compile a list of 500 pictures painted by Murillo, the greater part in the third or "vaporoso" manner, and painted in the last twenty-five years of his life. Had he not received the commission from Cadiz, or had he refused to accept it, we may suppose that his output would have been considerably greater than it was, for he was in excellent health, was a conscientious worker, and was painting his finest pictures. He has enabled us to know what manner of man he was by the records of his life, by his work, and by several portraits of himself that he painted. Two are in England. One of the painter in his youth was bought by Sir Francis Cook at the Louis Philippe sale in 1853, and is now at Doughty House; another painted in later years is in Lord Spencer's famous collection at Althorp. There are said to be others on the Continent; one, said by those who have seen it to be the best of all, was formerly in the Louvre, but its present resting-place is not known to the writer. The artist suffers to-day from the fact that Velazquez was his contemporary, and from the indiscriminate praise of those who became acquainted with him for the first time when Soult came back from the wars. His panegyrists ignored or never saw his weakness, the theatrical posing of his figures, the ever-recurring sacrifice of reason to sentiment, of strength to prettiness. His detractors, on the other hand, have blinded themselves to the beauty of his conceptions, the skill of his compositions, the exquisite quality of his colouring, and the spirit of genuine belief that kept a subject from becoming hackneyed, even when he had painted it a score of times. He did repeat himself; if we are not mistaken he has more than a score of canvases known to-day, setting out the story of the Immaculate Conception. The writer has seen some ten or twelve in Spain and France, and though the treatment is fairly uniform, each has been the object of the artist's most meticulous handling; indeed, it is on this account that the central figure lacks the charm that comes to the little angels clinging round her.

Murillo must have loved little children; he is never so happy and free from his besetting sin of posing figures stiffly as when he turns for inspiration to the little ones. We have several examples of this branch of his art in and round London. The National Gallery holds the "Drinking Boy," while Dulwich has several groups of beggar children and the delightful "Flower Girl." One may remark in passing that it is a thousand pities that the beauties of the Dulwich Collection are so little known to the general body of picture lovers. It can be reached on foot in two hours from the Bank of England, and is served by bus and train. Nearly all the Murillos are early ones, and the Velazquez (Philip IV.) is not altogether above suspicion, but the collection is a remarkable one, and sadly neglected by the public. It has often been urged against the Murillo children at Dulwich that they exhibit the painter's sin of theatrical posing in a very glaring light, but surely those who make this charge have overlooked the extraordinary self-consciousness of the Spanish beggar be he old or young. For once Murillo is justified. Among the beggars of Spain, rags that only hold together by grace of Providence are worn as though they were purple and fine linen; and the writer has seen the outcast, whose only possession beyond his rags was the cigarette that had just been given him, swagger along a dusty country high-road as though he were a grandee in electric motor passing through the ranks of his friends in the Park by the Prado when Madrid is in full season. There is much justification for the pose of the beggar children, the serious blame that attaches to the painter is for treating his divinities and saints as though they were no whit better than the exquisites of Sierpes or the beggars of the Macarena. Even his lambs are profoundly conscious that they are sitting for their portrait, and have made up their mind that if they are spared to grow up and become sheep they will be worthy of their pastures. The painter was not justified in this, although we must never forget, if we would do him justice, that the Church kept a watchful eye on everything he did, and spoke to him with an authority he would have been the last to disregard. The Catholic Church is essentially spectacular in its worship, and surely the high dignitaries of the seventeenth-century Church would never have suffered Murillo to go unrebuked had he presented his figures in simpler pose and without any ostentation in their attitude. As things were he had brought the Godhead dangerously close to earth.

Our entire conception of the province of art has altered beyond recognition since Murillo lived and died. The modern artist, whether he work with paint or words, keeps his morality and his art distinct from one another. Art, he says, is not concerned with a rule of life, it is essentially non-moral. Murillo, on the other hand, accepted the theory that art is the handmaiden of the Church, that only the handling of the chosen picture is the affair of the painter. Where faith was concerned he was not far removed from Beato Angelico, and those who like to compare the products of an age in different countries, may remember that Carlo Dolci, the Florentine painter of cardinal virtues, was born about the same time as Murillo. The Church did for him in Italy what it did for Murillo in Spain, but the latter artist was made of sterner stuff, and had infinitely more brains and talent than his Florentine contemporary. But between Carlo Dolci's best work and Murillo's worst, there is a measure of resemblance that justifies one in remembering that they were born within a year of each other, and that both passed in the penultimate decade of the seventeenth century.

In conclusion it may be said for Murillo that, quite apart from his merits as a man, he may claim the admiration of the unbiassed critic of all time for some of his finest pictures. There were occasions when he painted figures that neither Velazquez nor Titian would have felt ashamed to own, there were times when his saints and Redeemer were expressed with exquisite dignity and restraint. Judged by the light of modern criticism, he was uneven in his work, but that criticism has no reason to believe that its arguments would have conveyed anything to

Murillo himself. His entire output suggests that he knew what his message was to be, and delivered it as he received it. We can find pictures in which the proportions of the figures are bad, and the outlines are hard and unpleasing, there are a few in which the colour scheme is poor and ineffective. But if against his worst moments we are content to put his best, the artist has not much to fear. Apart from the value of his labours on purely artistic grounds, let us remember that he brought the Madonna and Infant Christ from the Heaven in which they had been inaccessible to the rank and file of Spain, to the earth where they might be seen and known, by those who walk in darkness.

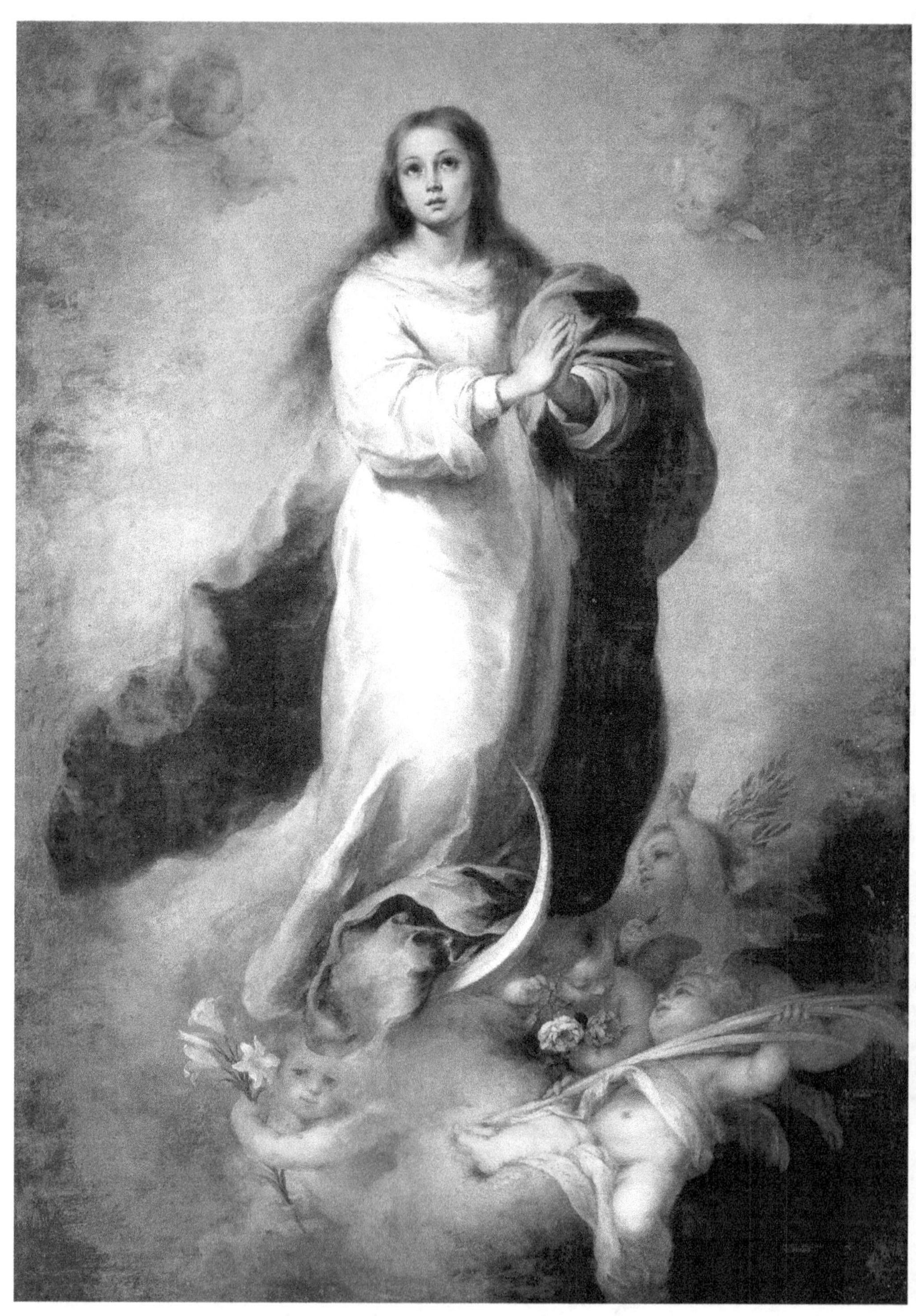

B.E. Murillo, The Immaculate Conception, 1660-65, Prado

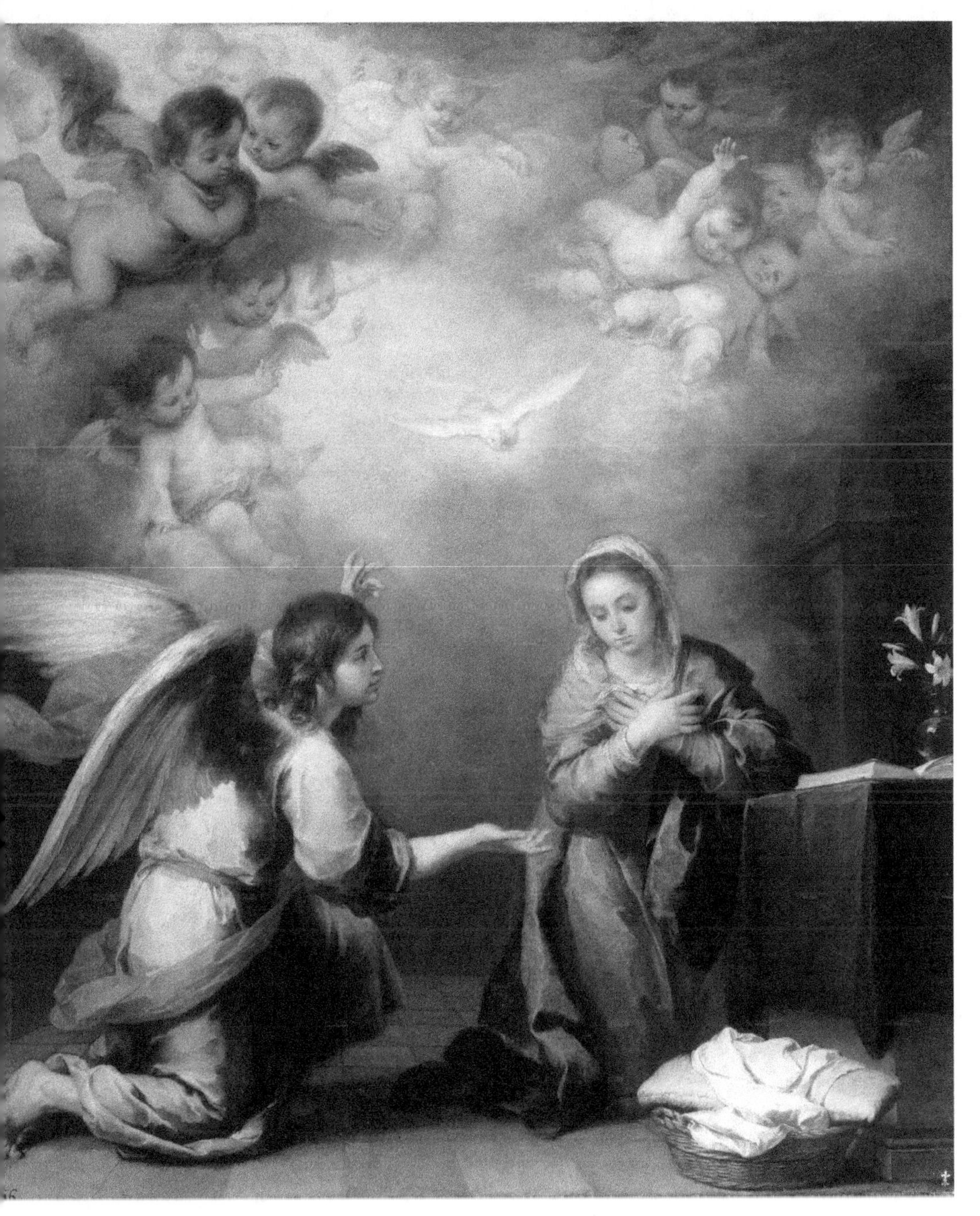

B.E. Murillo, The Annunciation, 1660-65, Prado

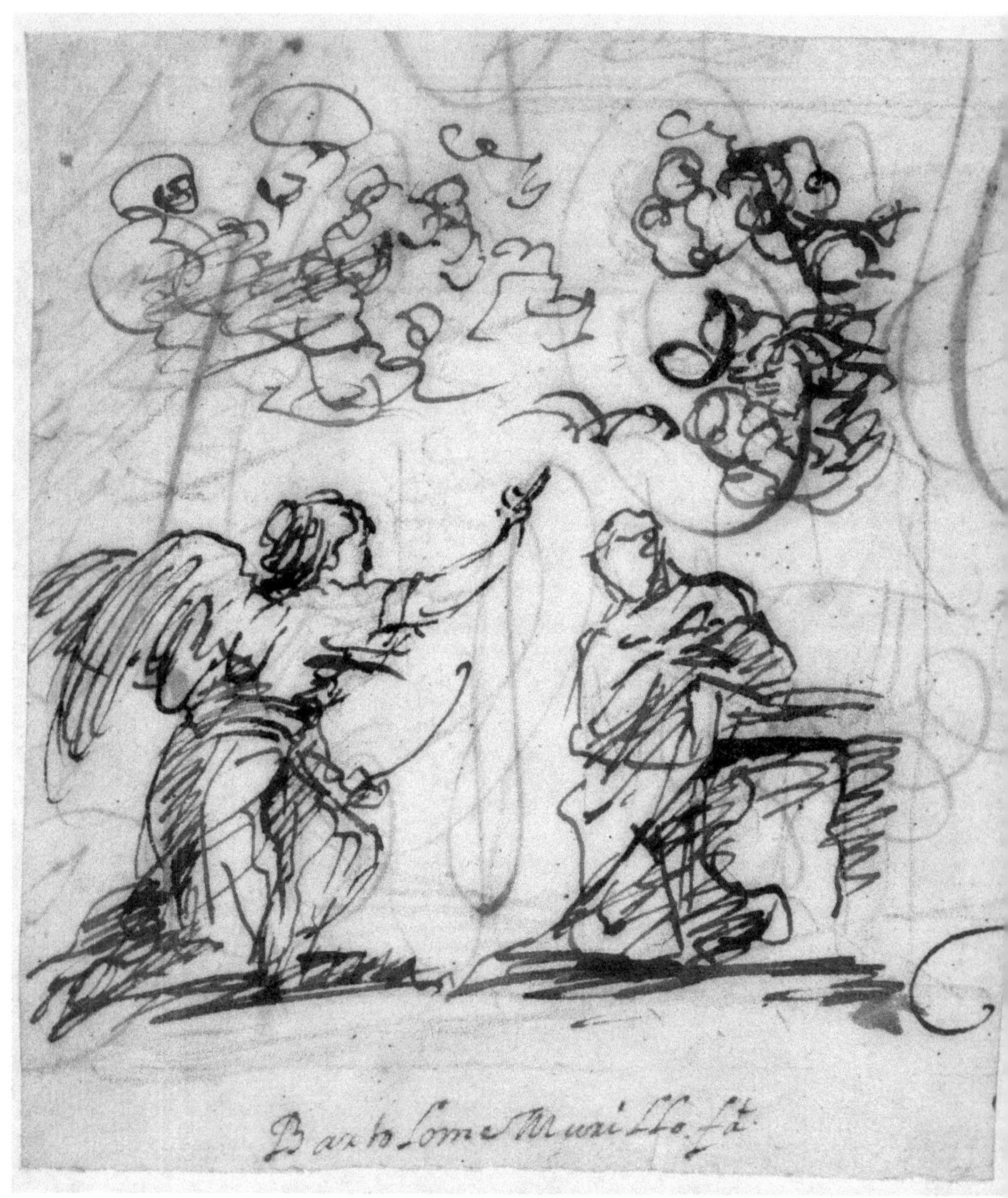

B.E. Murillo, Annunciation, study, 1650

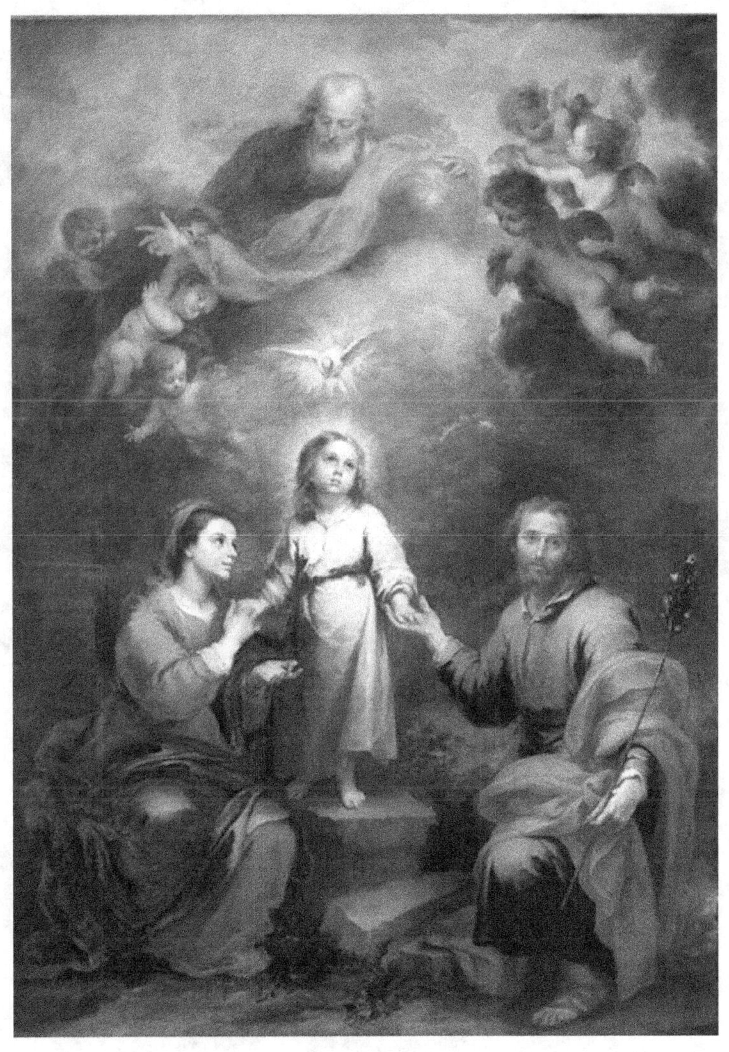

B.E. Murillo, The Holy Family,
1675-82, National Gallery, London

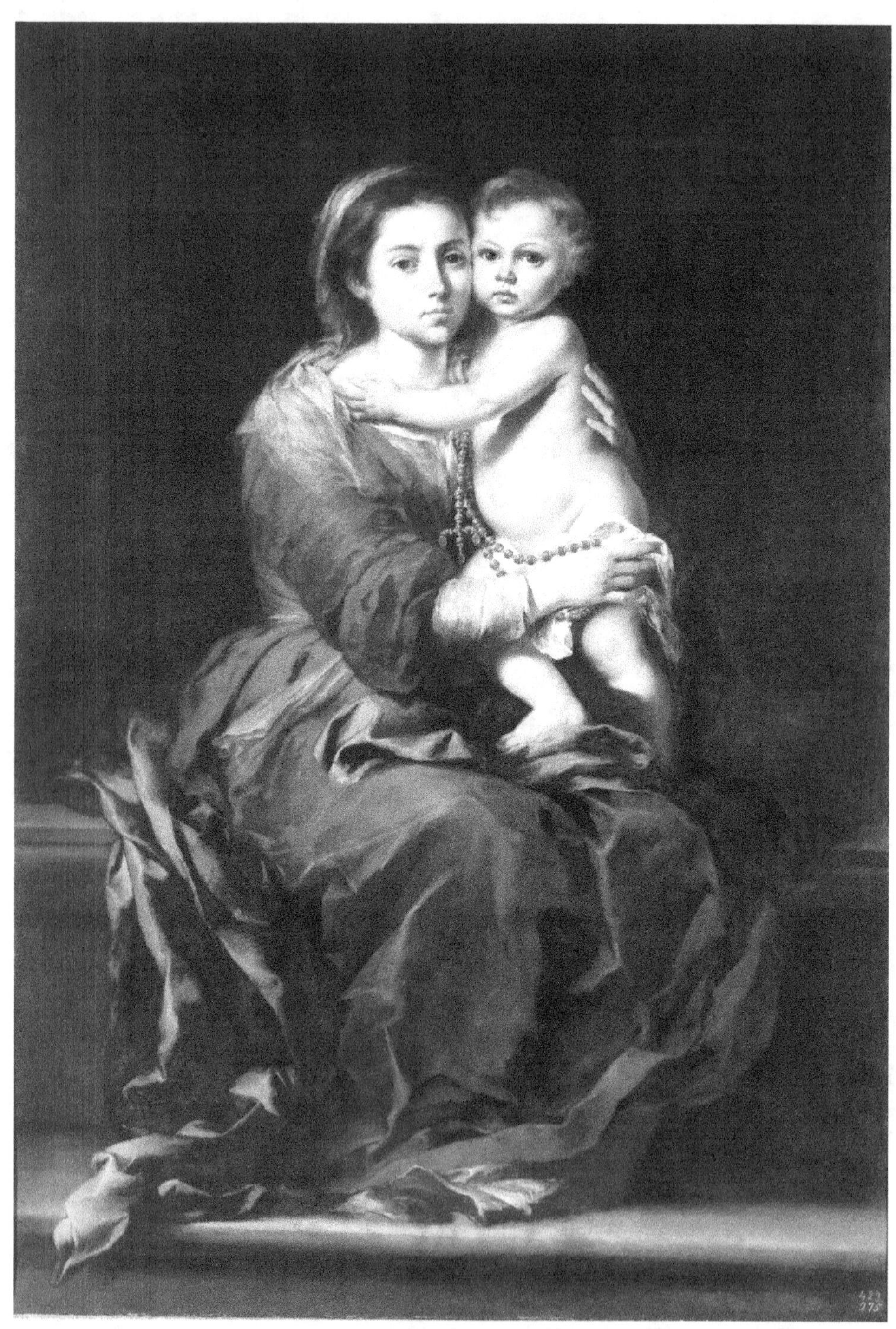

B.E.Murillo, Madonna and Child, 1660-65, Prado

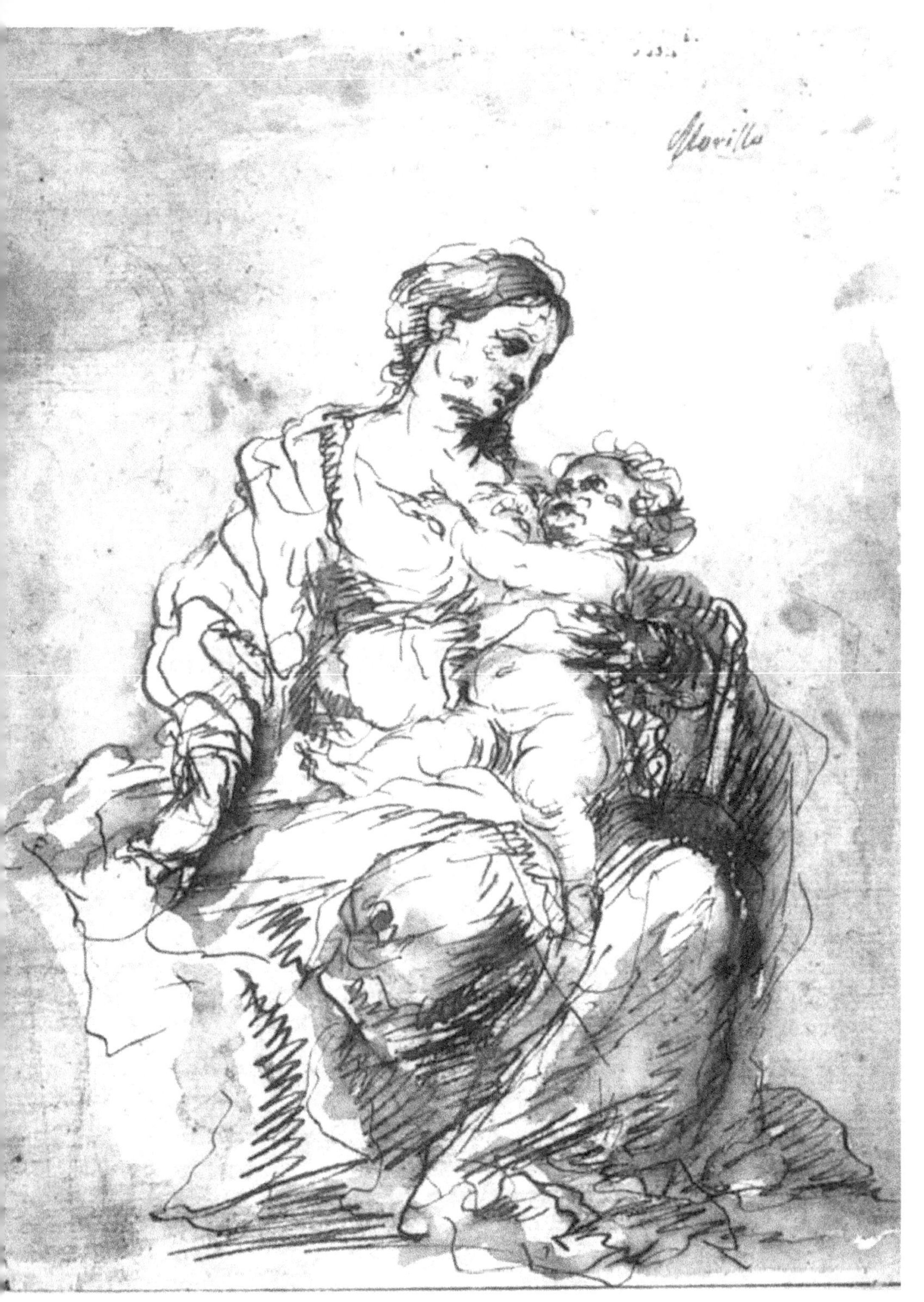

Bartolomé Murillo, Virgin and Child, Cleveland

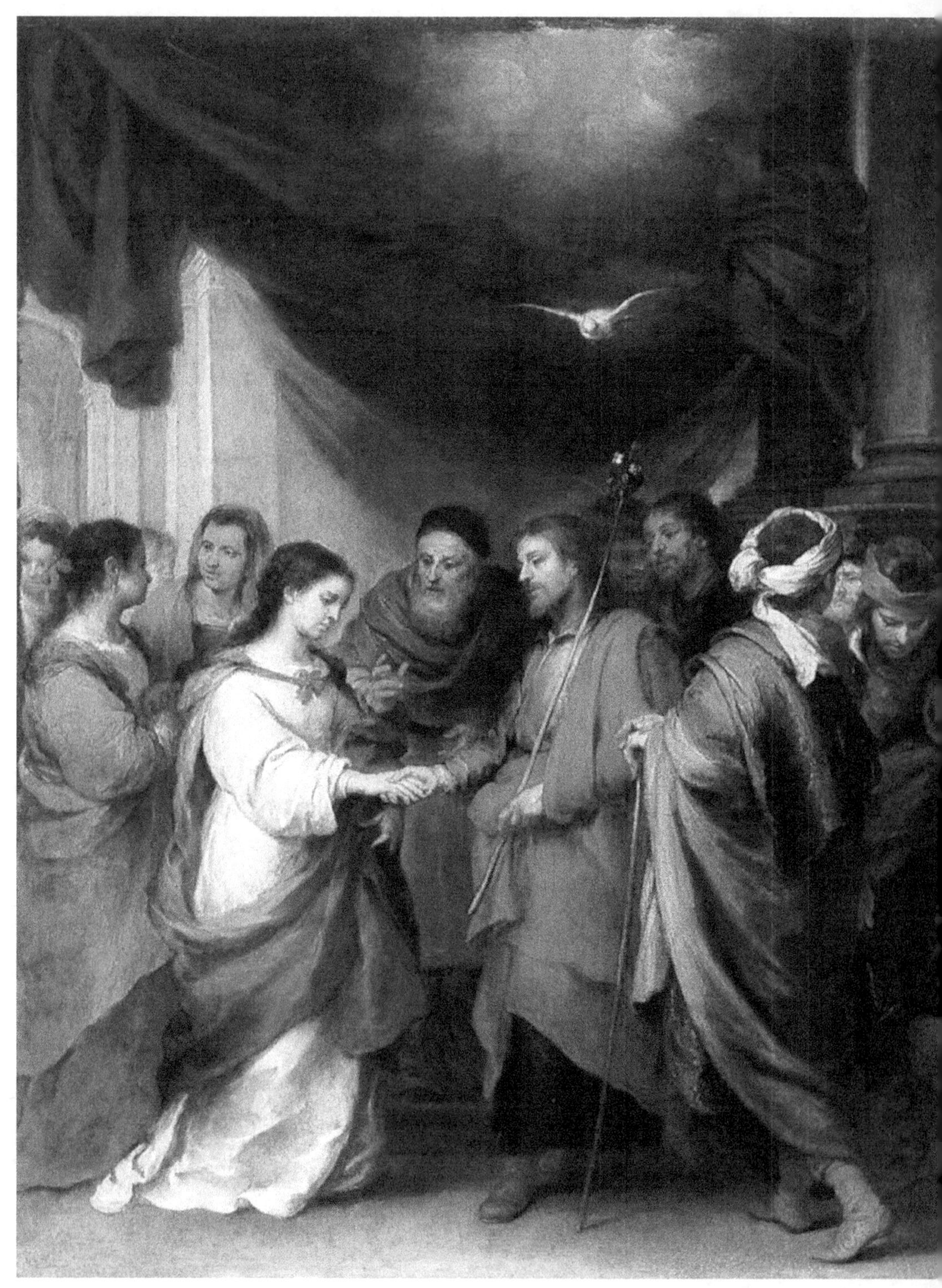

B.E. Murillo, The Marriage of the Virgin, 1670, Wallace Collection

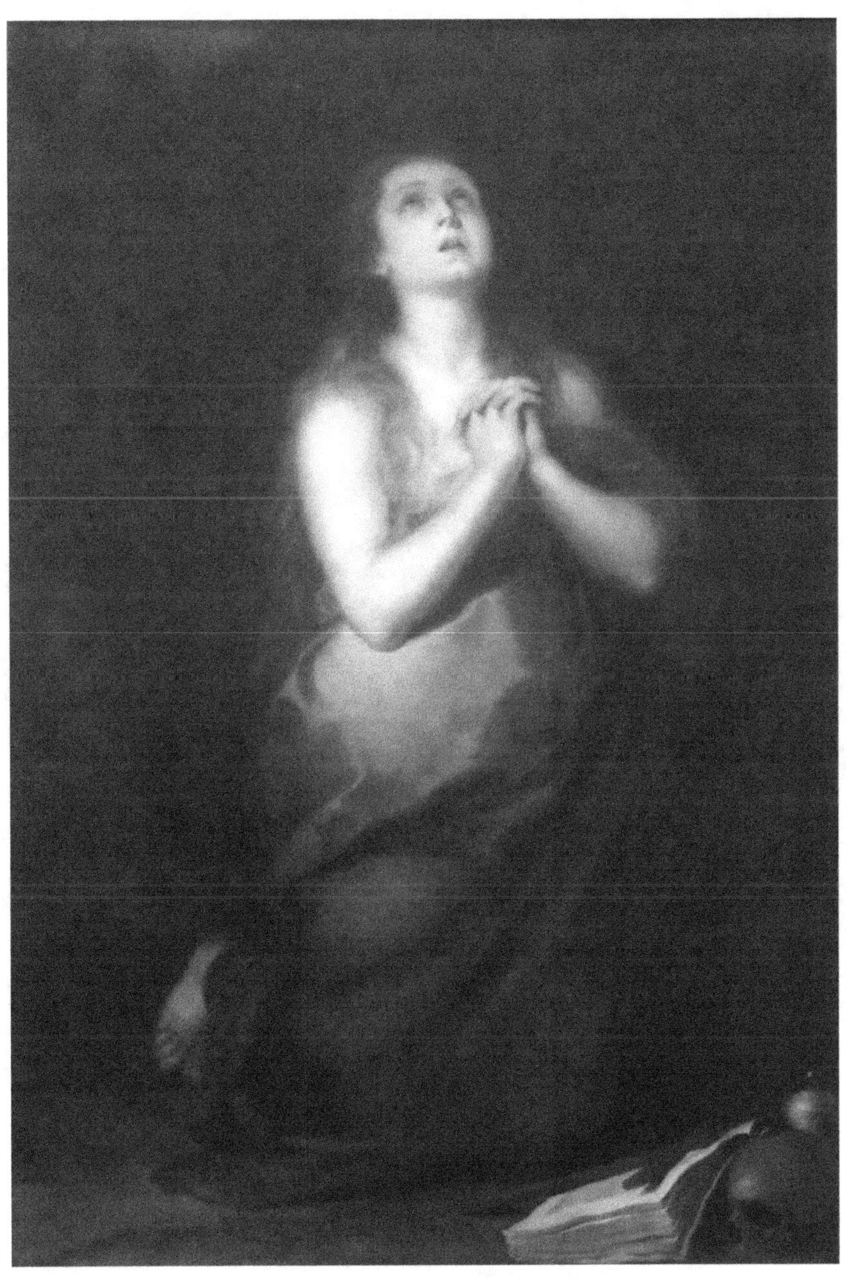

B.E. Murillo, Mary Magdalene, 1660-65, San Diego Museum of Art

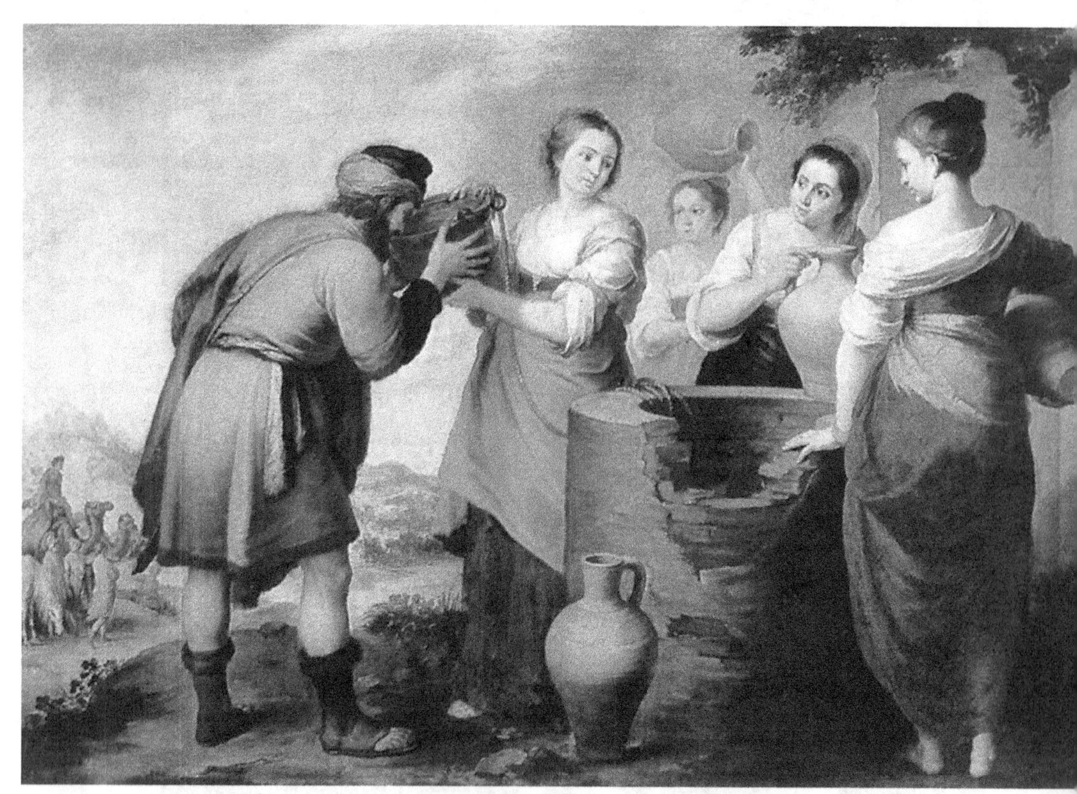

B.E. Murillo, Rebecca and Elieze, 1660, Prado

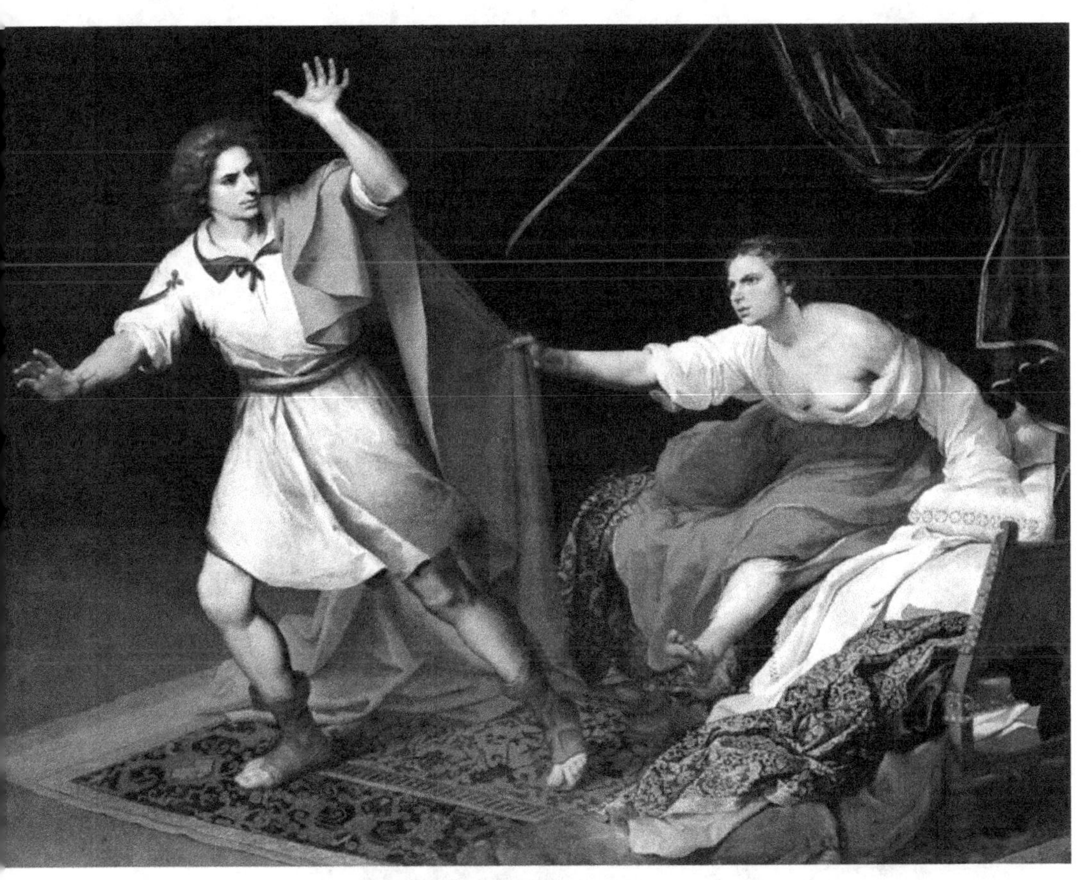

B.E. Murillo, Joseph and Potiphar's Wife, 1640-45, Kassel

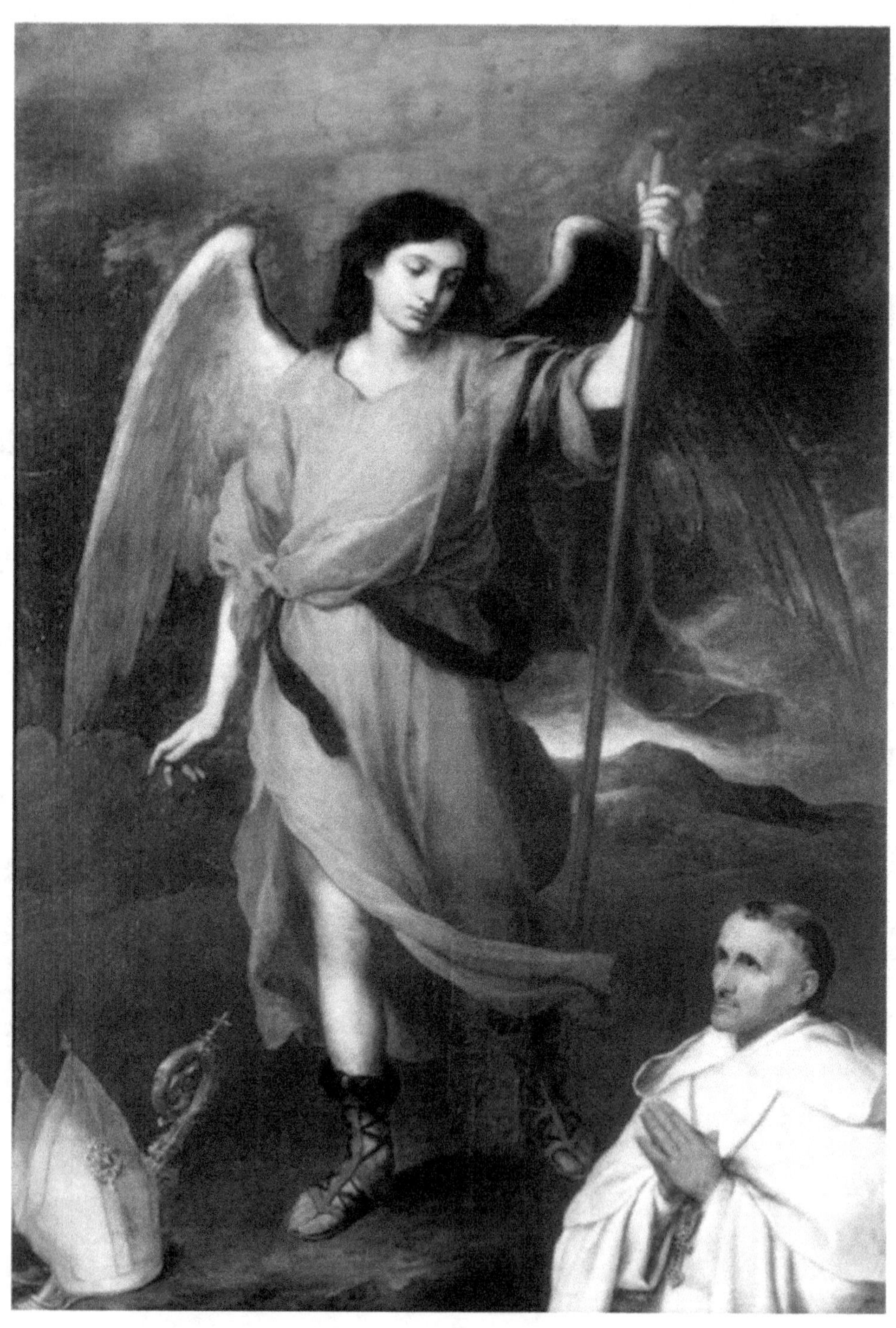

B.E. Murillo, Archangel Raphael and Bishop Domonte, Museum Pushkin

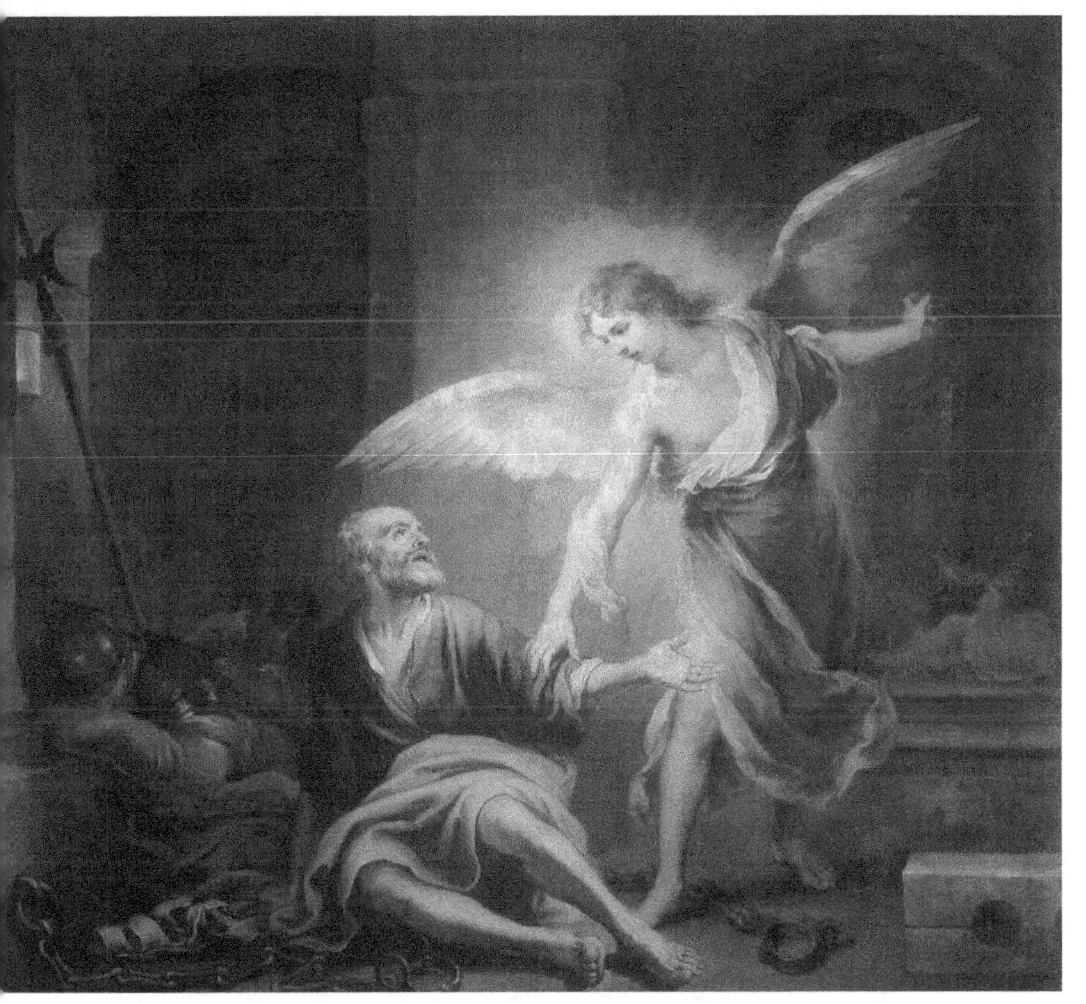

B.E. Murillo, Liberacion de San Pedro, 1665-57, Hermitage Museum

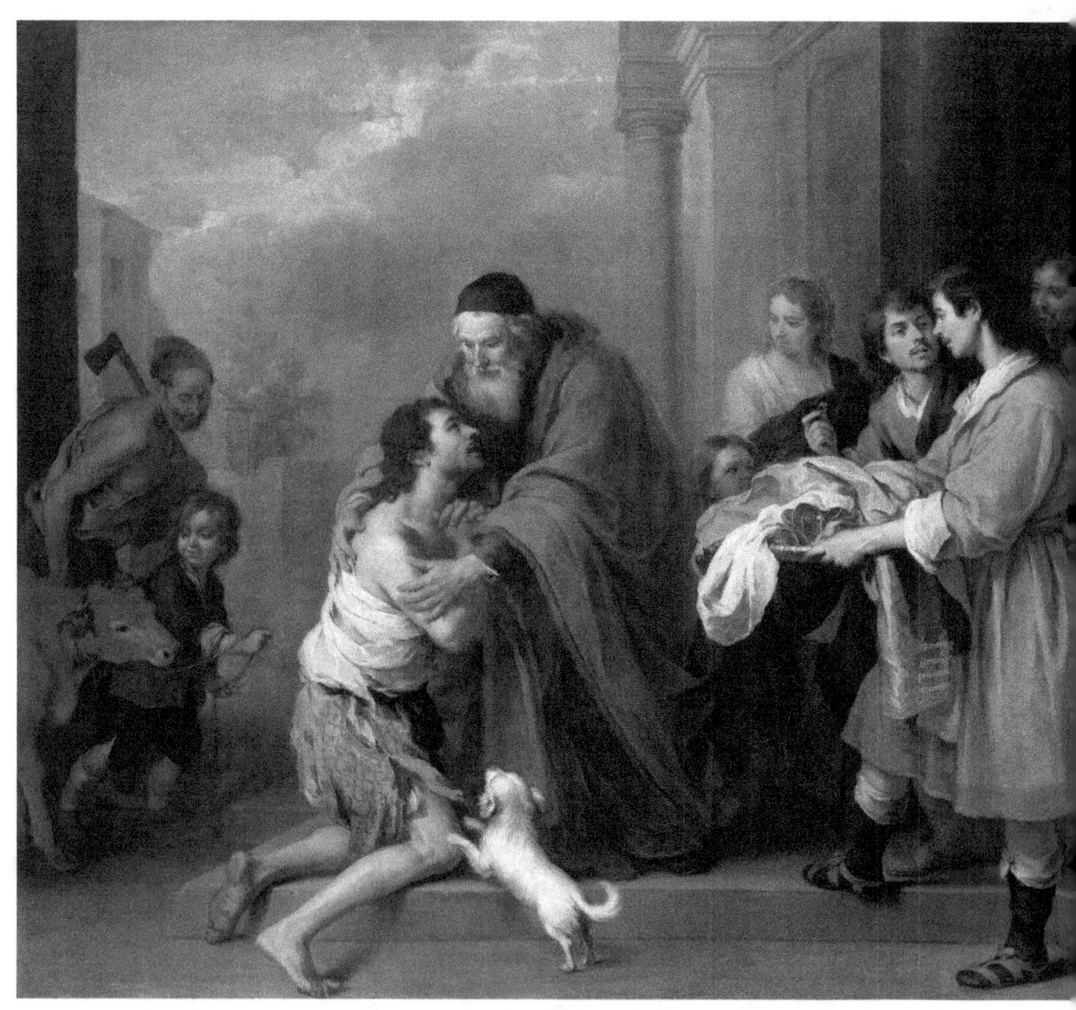

B.E. Murillo, The Return of the Prodigal Son,
1667-1670, National Gallery, Washington, DC

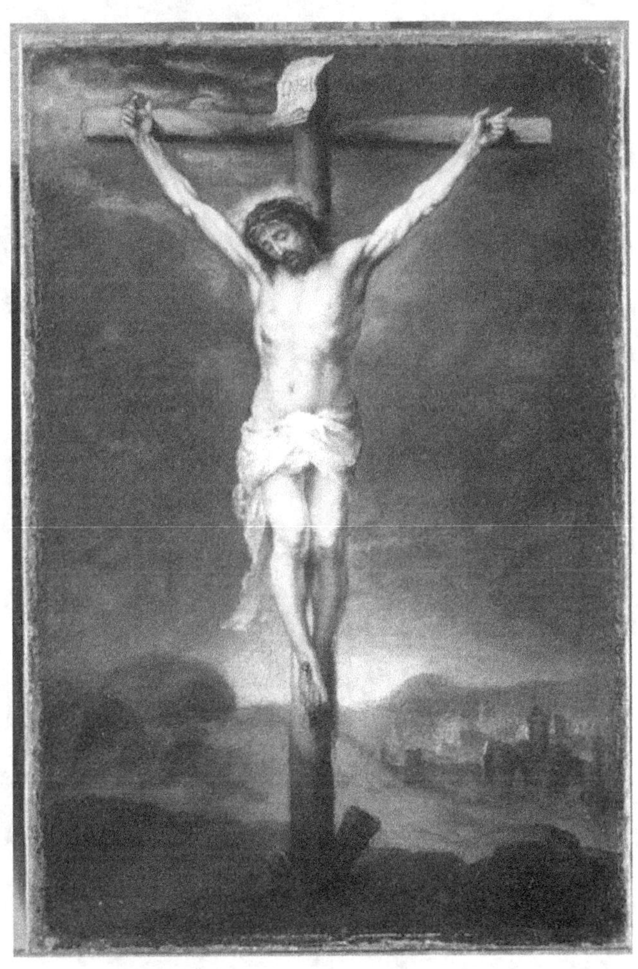

B.E. Murillo, Crucifixion, 1675, Metropolitan Museum,
New York City

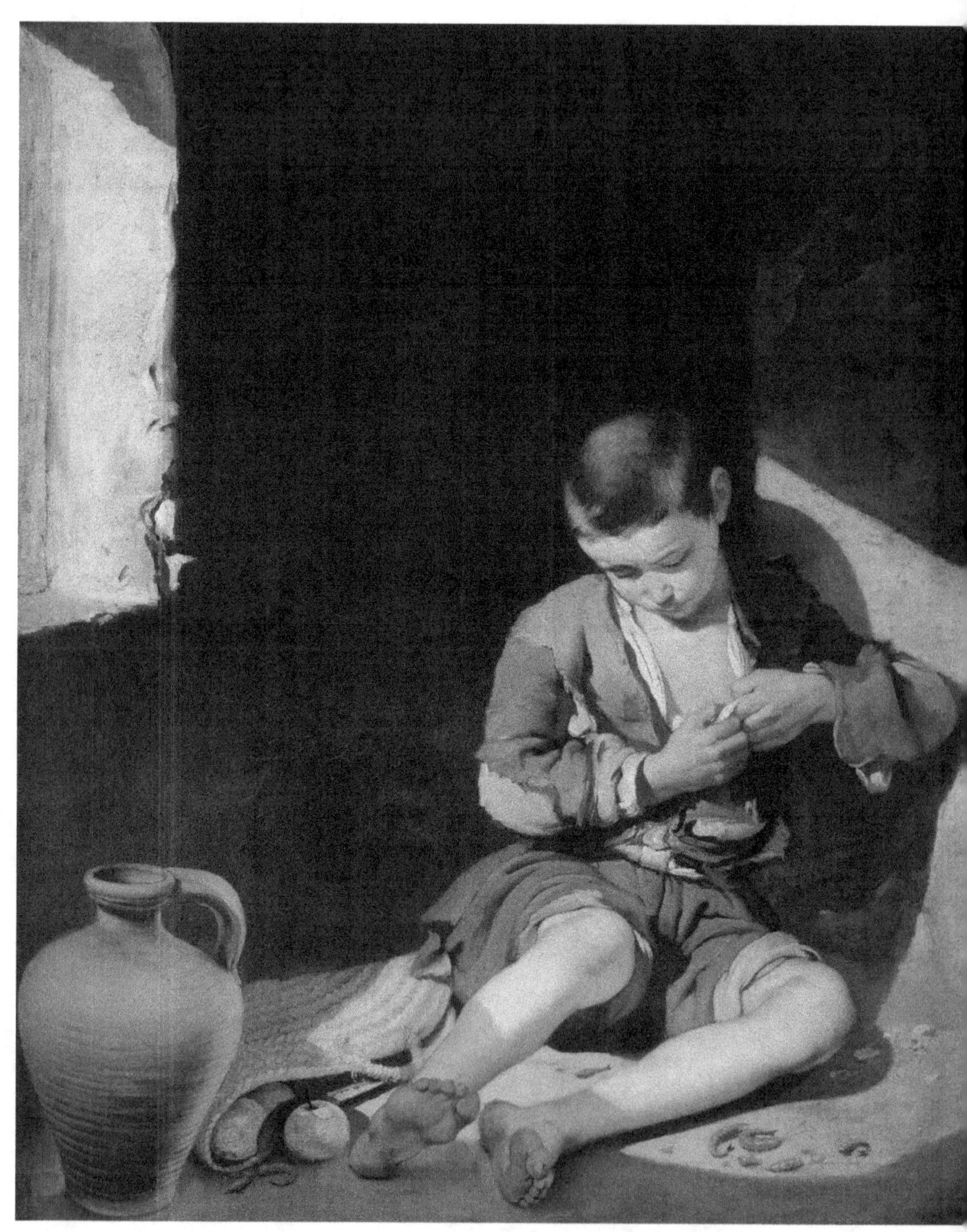

B.E. Murillo, The Young Beggar, 1665, Louvre

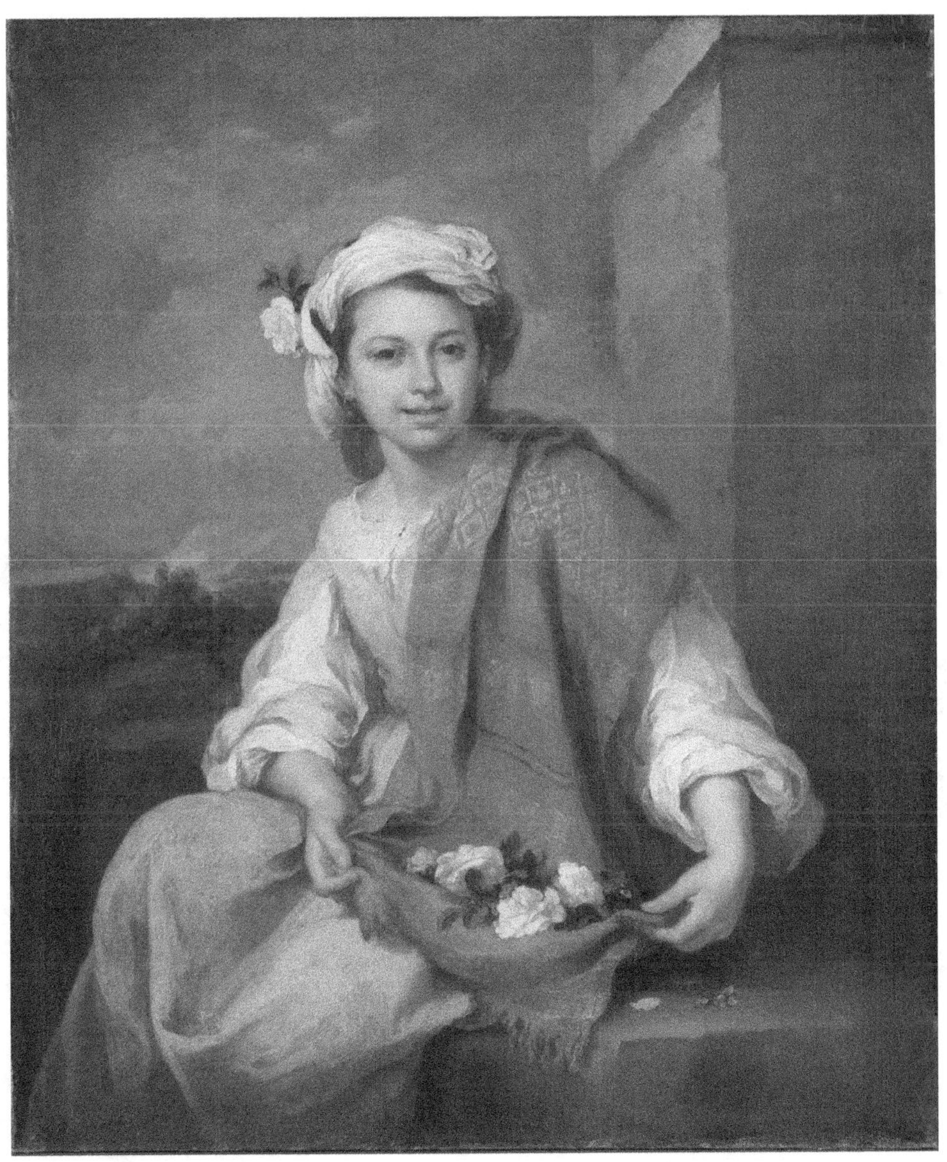

B.E. Murillo, The Flower Girl, 1665-70, London

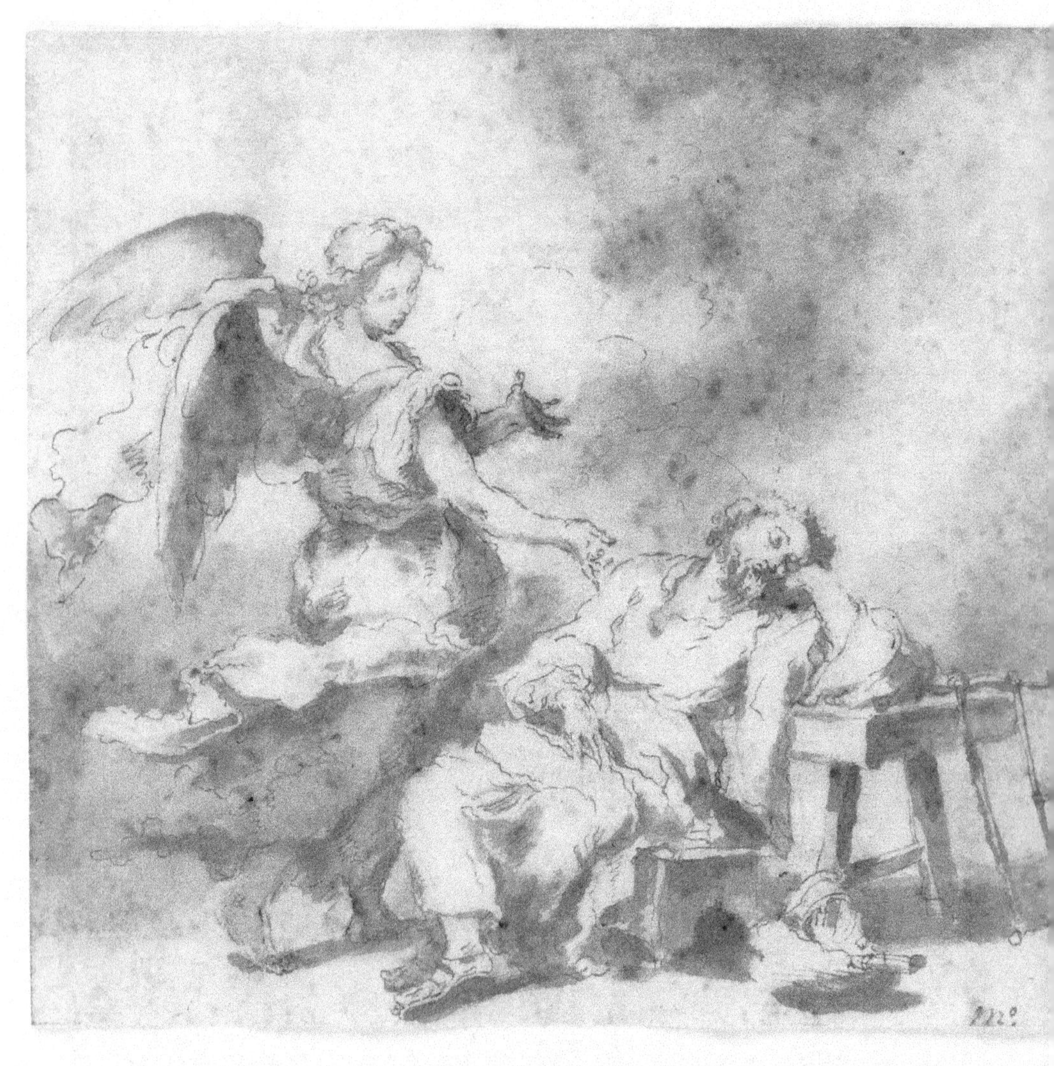

B.E. Murillo, The Dream of St Joseph, 1668-82, Prado

NOTES ON THE ILLUSTRATIONS

PLATE I. - THE IMMACULATE CONCEPTION..
(From the Louvre, Paris)

This greatly admired canvas is one of the painter's many studies of a familiar subject. There are more than a dozen pictures of the Immaculate Conception whose authenticity is undisputed, and there are many others on offer in Spain, clever and sometimes old imitations of the master's mannerisms. In this case the figure of the Virgin is rather over-elaborated, but the treatment of the attendant cherubs is delightful and the composition very skilful.

PLATE II. - THE BEGGAR GIRL
(From the Dulwich Gallery)

We should prefer to call this picture the Flower-seller, for the girl is not really a beggar at all. Her clothes are worn with some approach to nicety, and she carries roses that command a ready sale in Seville if the seller be attractive and young. Murillo has given us a very charming type of Spanish girl, and has obtained some striking colour harmonies.

PLATE III. - THE HOLY FAMILY
(From the Louvre, Paris)

This is one of the masterpieces of the Paris collection, beautiful alike in conception, colouring and composition, with all the merits of the artist in evidence, and the most of his weaknesses conspicuous by their absence.

PLATE IV. - MADONNA OF THE ROSARY
(From the Dulwich Gallery)

The Virgin sits enthroned, with the Holy Child on her knee and attendant cherubs at her feet. Her expression is full of sadness. The composition is admirably thought out and the colouring effective.

PLATE V. - THE BEGGAR BOY
(From the Dulwich Gallery)

The little gallery near Dulwich College, some five miles away from the boundaries of the City of London, is rich in works by Murillo. This study of a beggar boy possesses more than the interest created by the artist's clever treatment of shadow and light, the happiness of the posing and the skilled brushwork. It reveals the truth that between the beggar of nigh three hundred years ago and to-day there is little or no difference in Spain. You may meet this child to-day in and round the Andalusian country the painter knew so well.

PLATE VI. – A BOY DRINKING
(From National Gallery, London)

When Murillo was not concerned with Virgin, Saints or Martyrs, he loved to turn to the picturesque types of childhood that he found in the streets around him. He has undoubtedly brought more character, more humanity, and above all more movement into his child-life studies than into his sacred pictures. The National Gallery is the fortunate possessor of one of the painter's most successful studies of children, reproduced here.

PLATE VII. – THE NATIVITY
(From the Louvre, Paris)

On several occasions Murillo chose the Nativity for the subject of his great canvases. He was always safe to attract the admiration of his clients by his reverent treatment of a scene that left so much to the imagination of the artist. His pictures were very greatly admired by the French invaders of Spain, and it was to Marshal Soult that many Frenchmen owed their first introduction to Murillo.

PLATE VIII. – THE MARRIAGE OF THE VIRGIN
(From the Wallace Collection)

This is a panel-picture of considerable merit, full of charm and very sincerely felt. As is customary with Murillo, the grouping is better than the colouring, which has a certain tendency to crudity, not altogether restrained by the limits of the canvas.

On the following pages are some illustrations of contemporaries of Murillo.

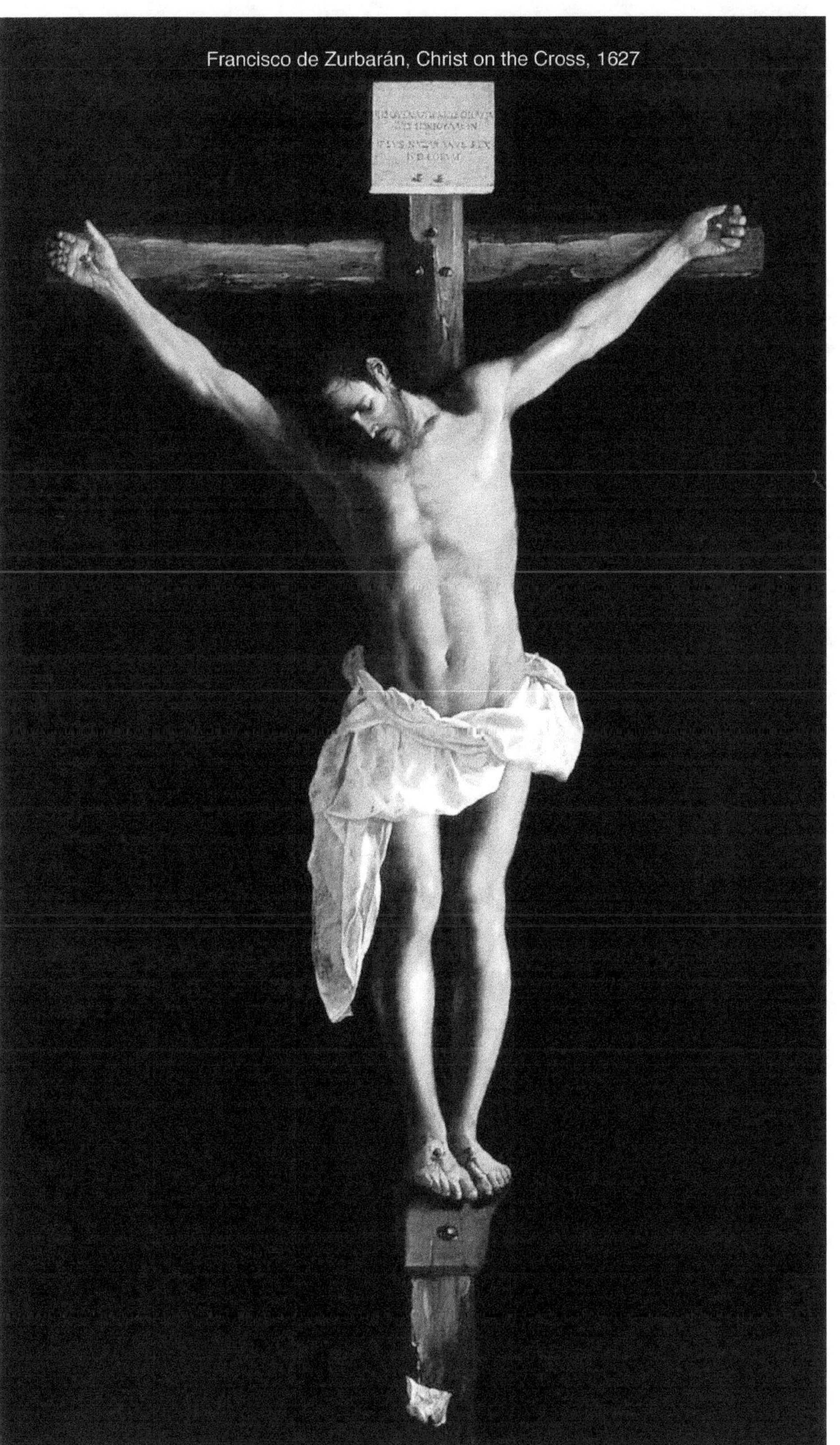

Francisco de Zurbarán, Christ on the Cross, 1627

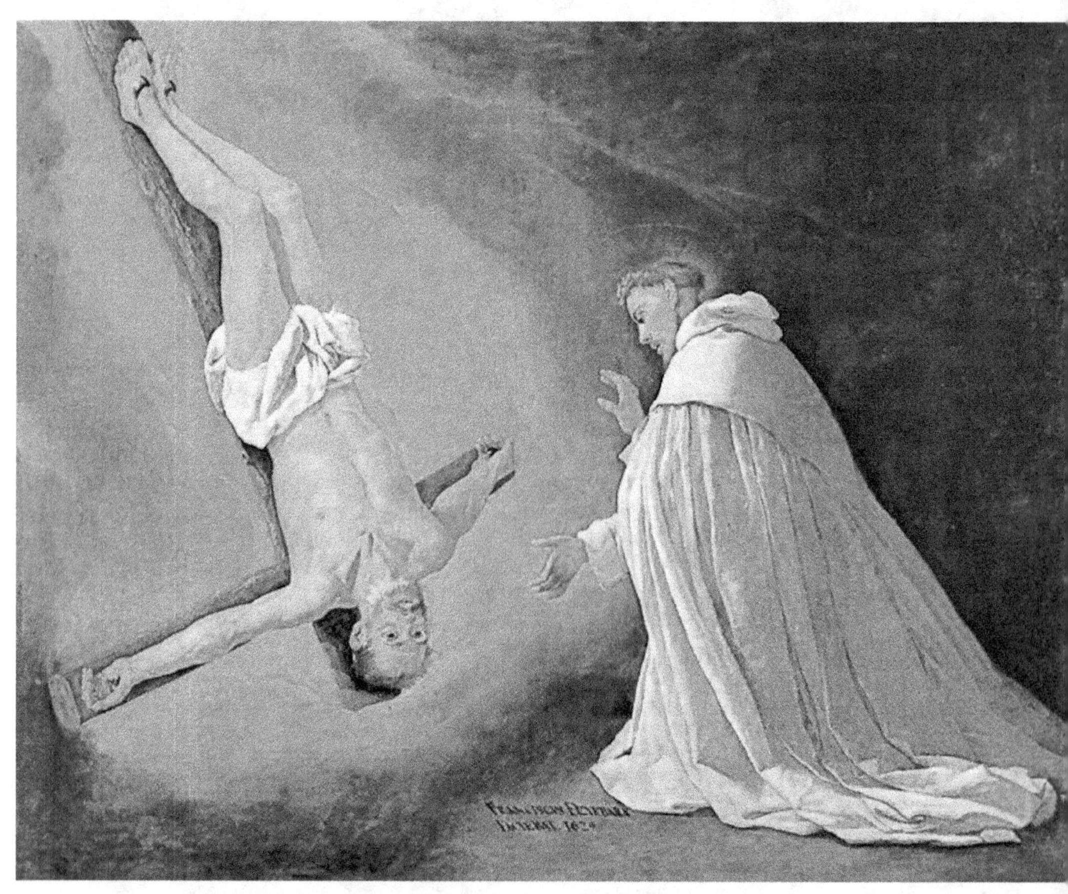

Francisco de Zurbarán,
The Apostle of St Peter Appearing to St Peter of Nolasco,
1629, Prado, Madrid

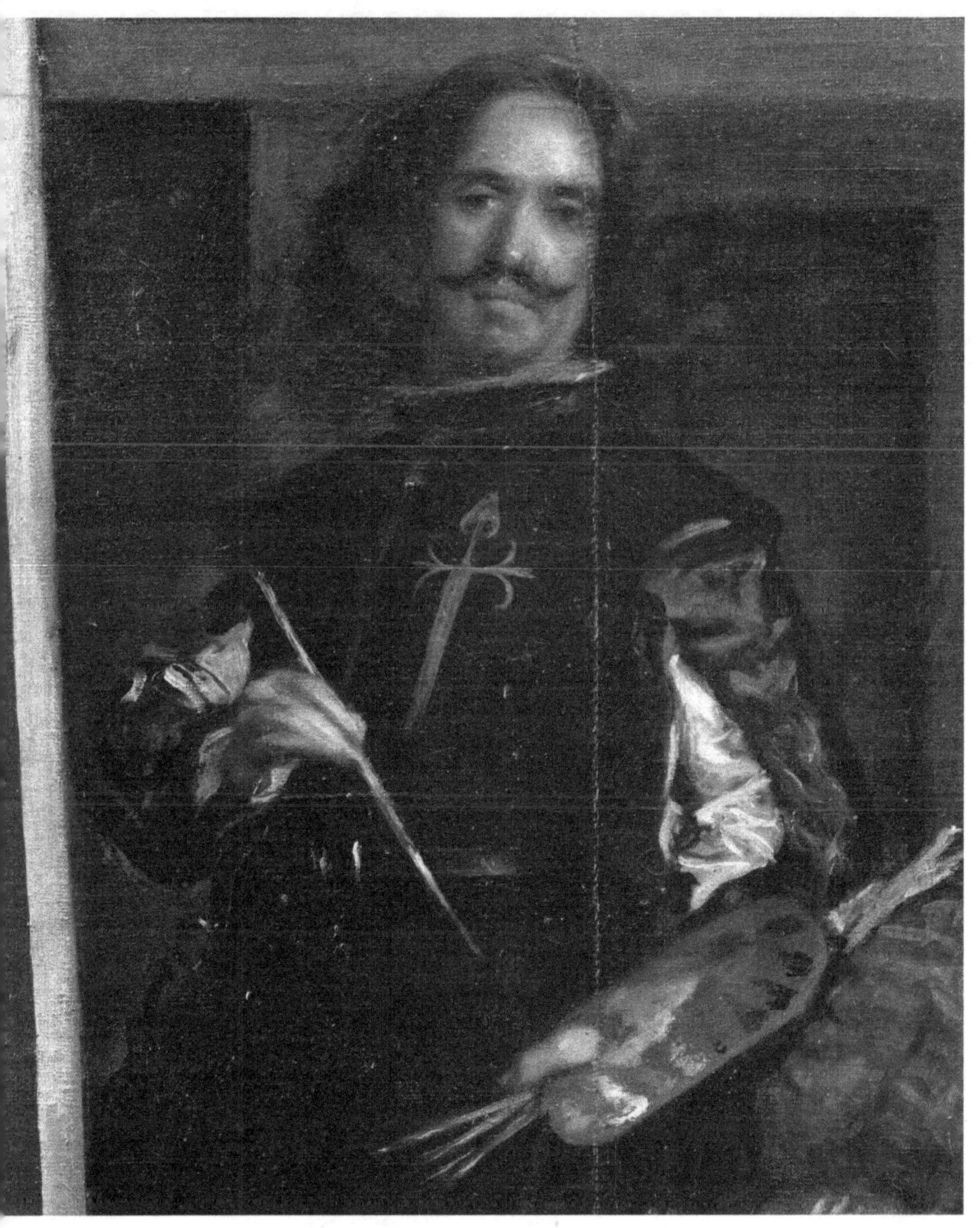

Diego Velásquez, detail of Las Meninas

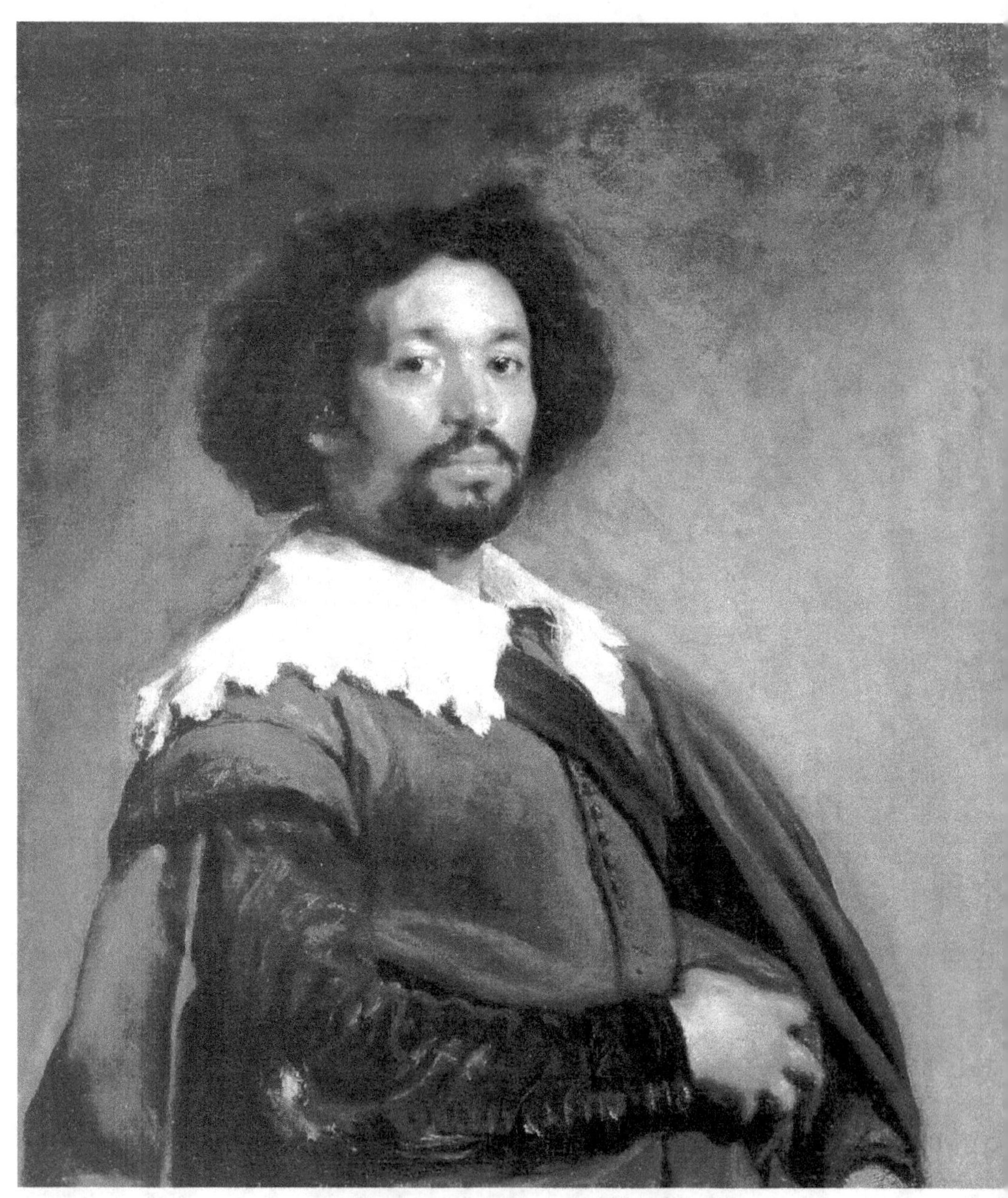

Diego de Velásquez, Juan de Pareja, 1650,
Metropolitan Museum of Art, New York

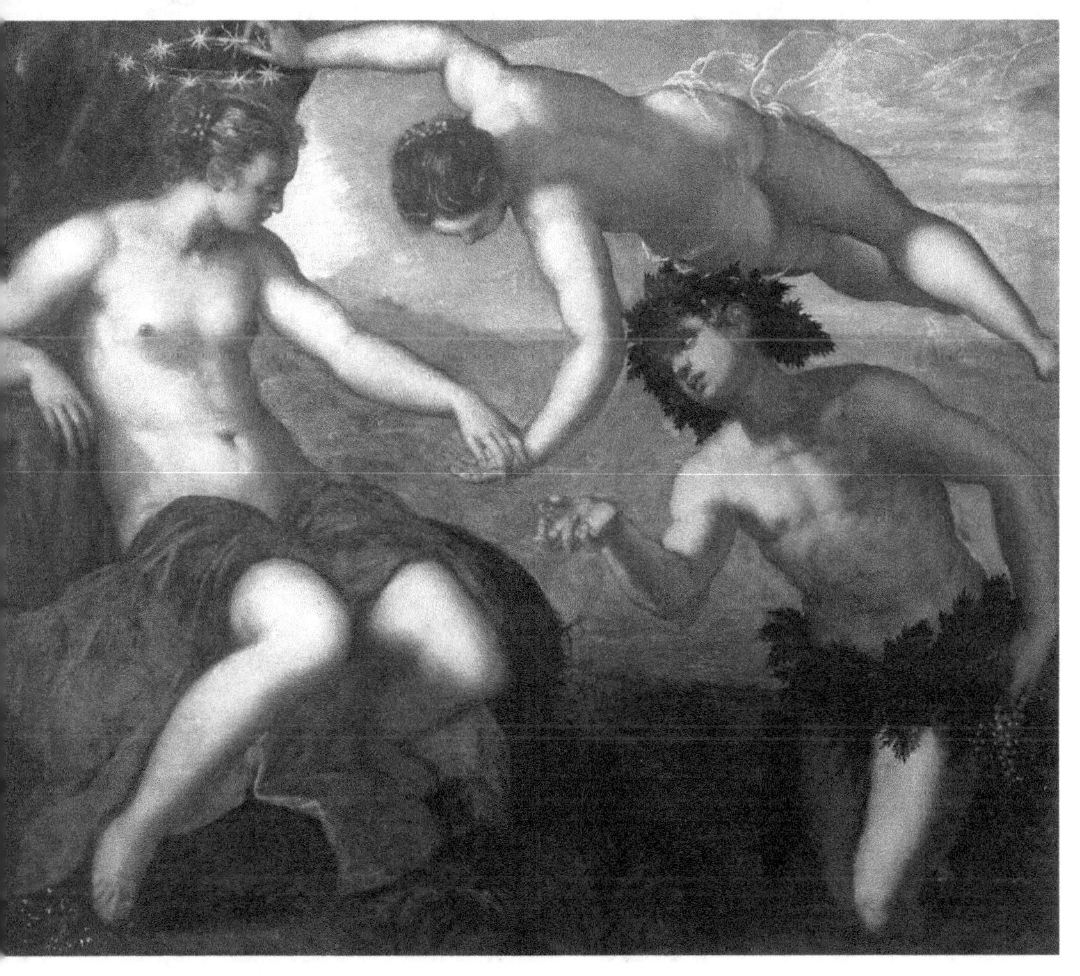

Tintoretto, Bacchus, Ariadne and Venus, 1576-77, Venice

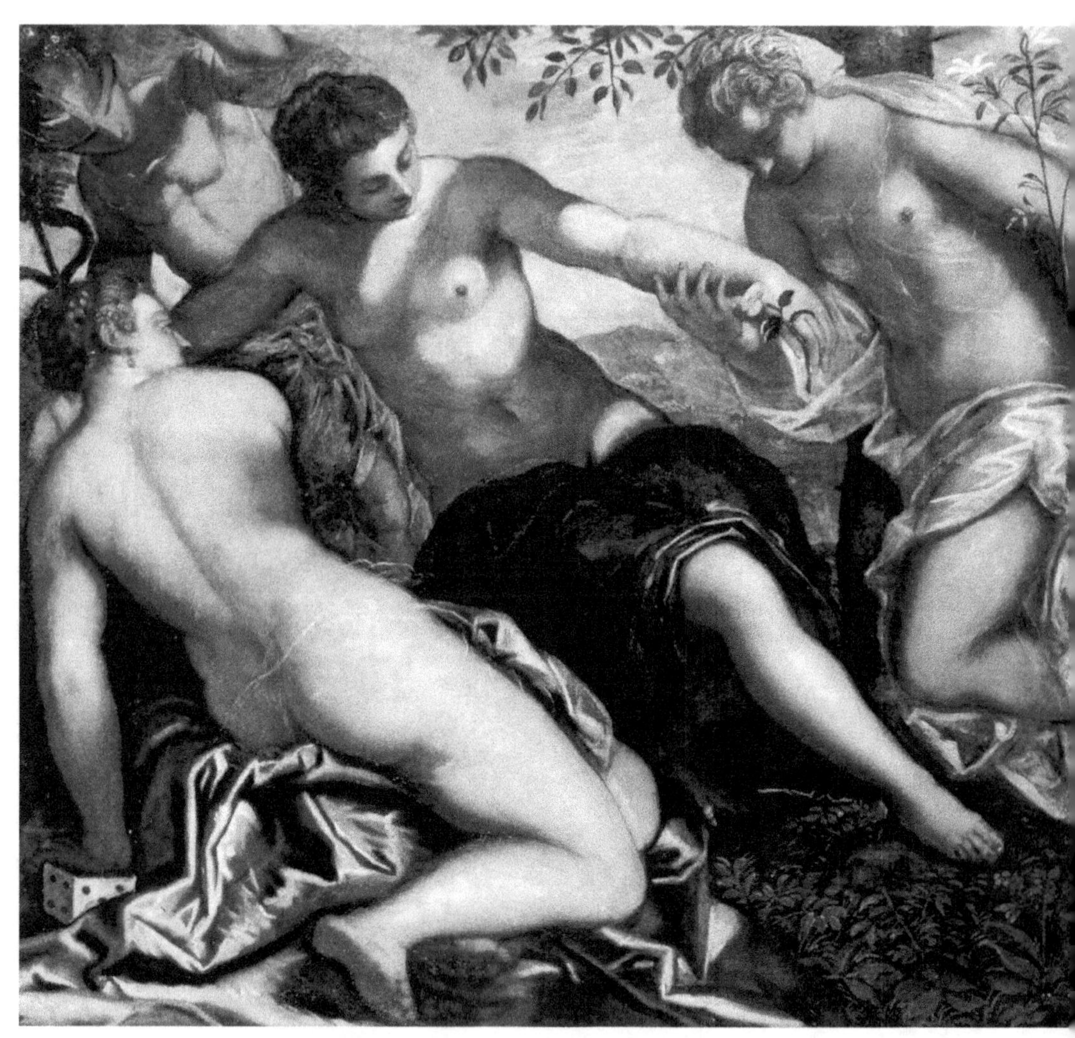

Jacopo Tintoretto, Mercury and the Graces, 1577

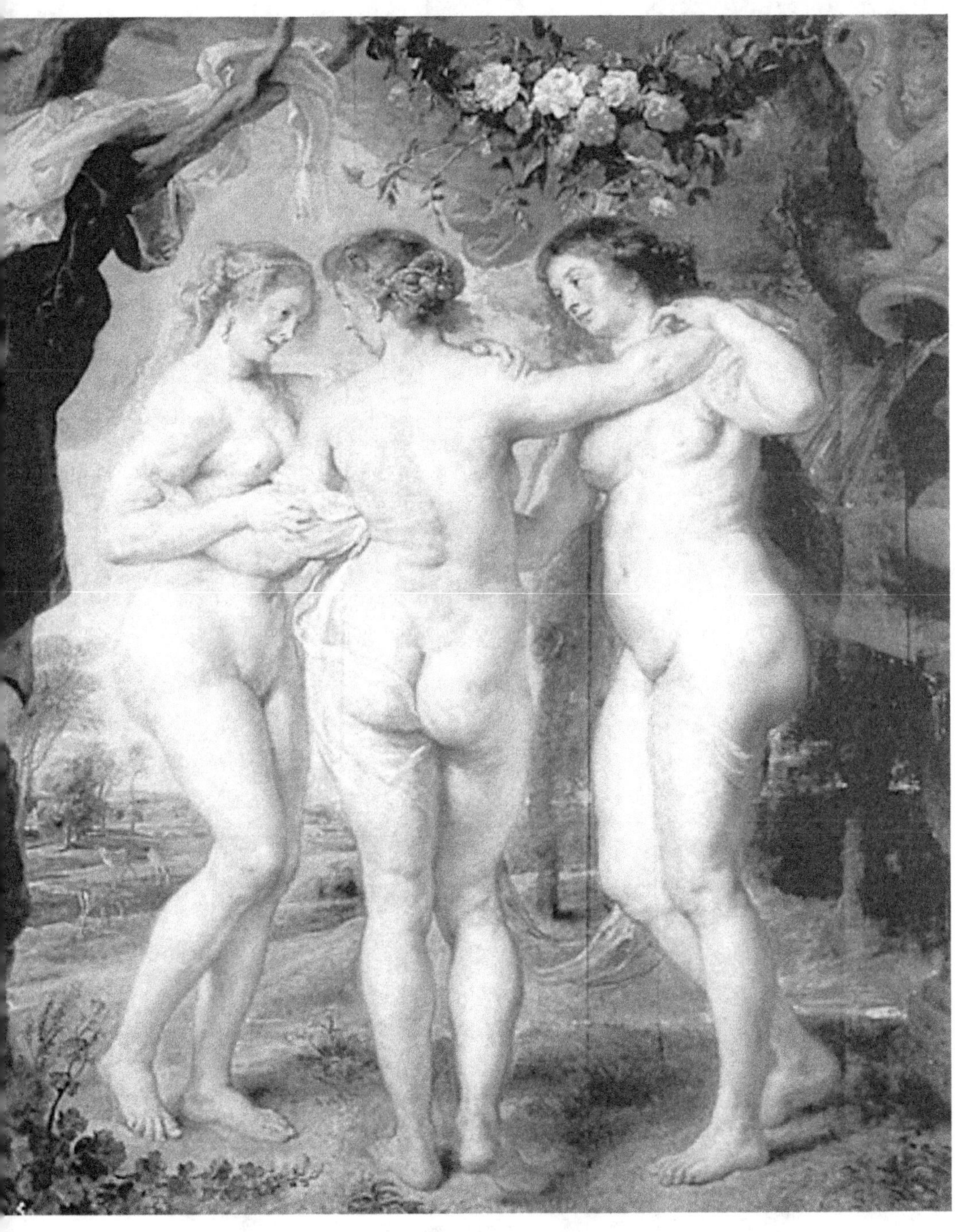

Peter Paul Rubens, The Three Graces, 1638-40, Prado, Madrid

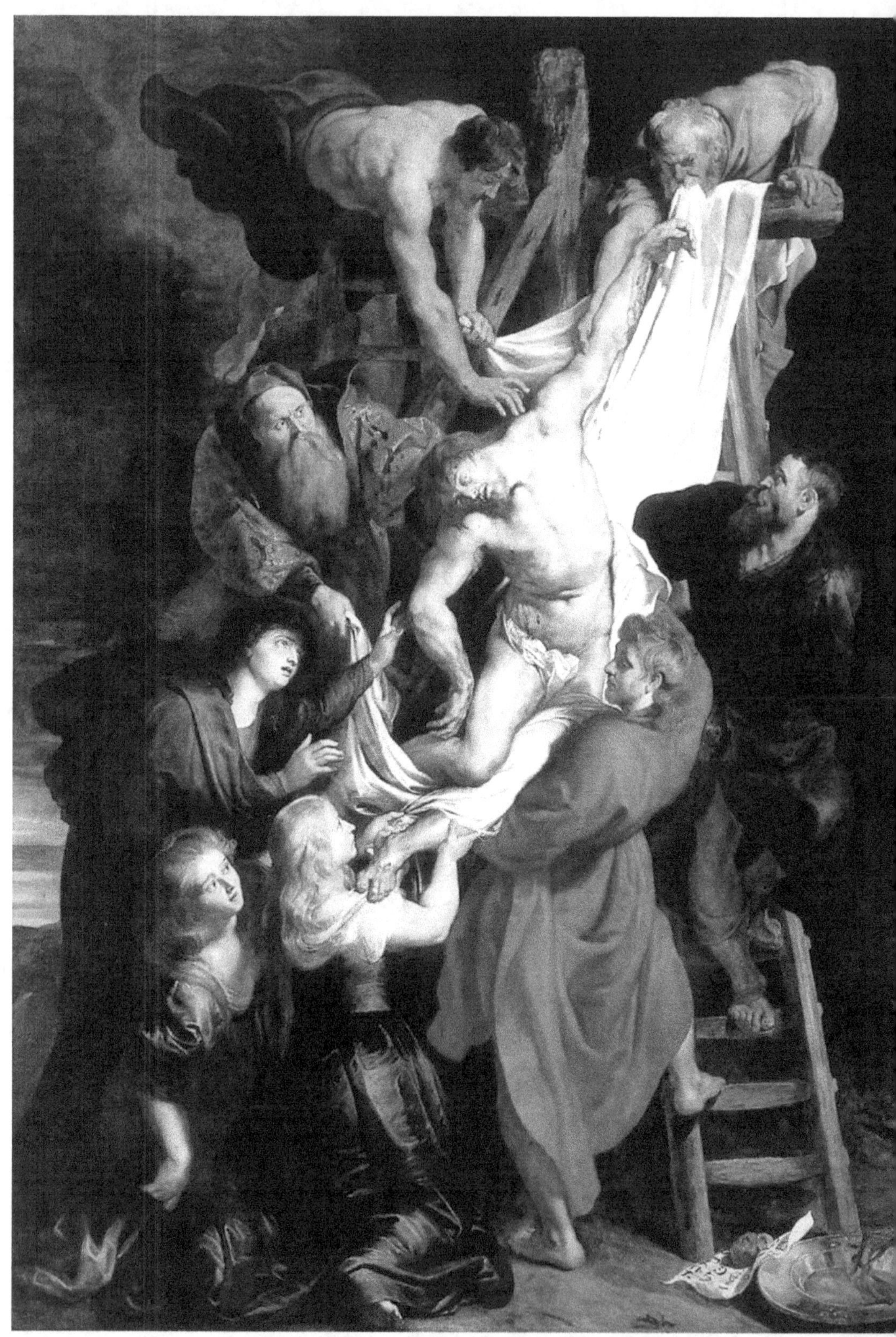

Peter Paul Rubens, Descent From the Cross, c. 1610, Antwerp

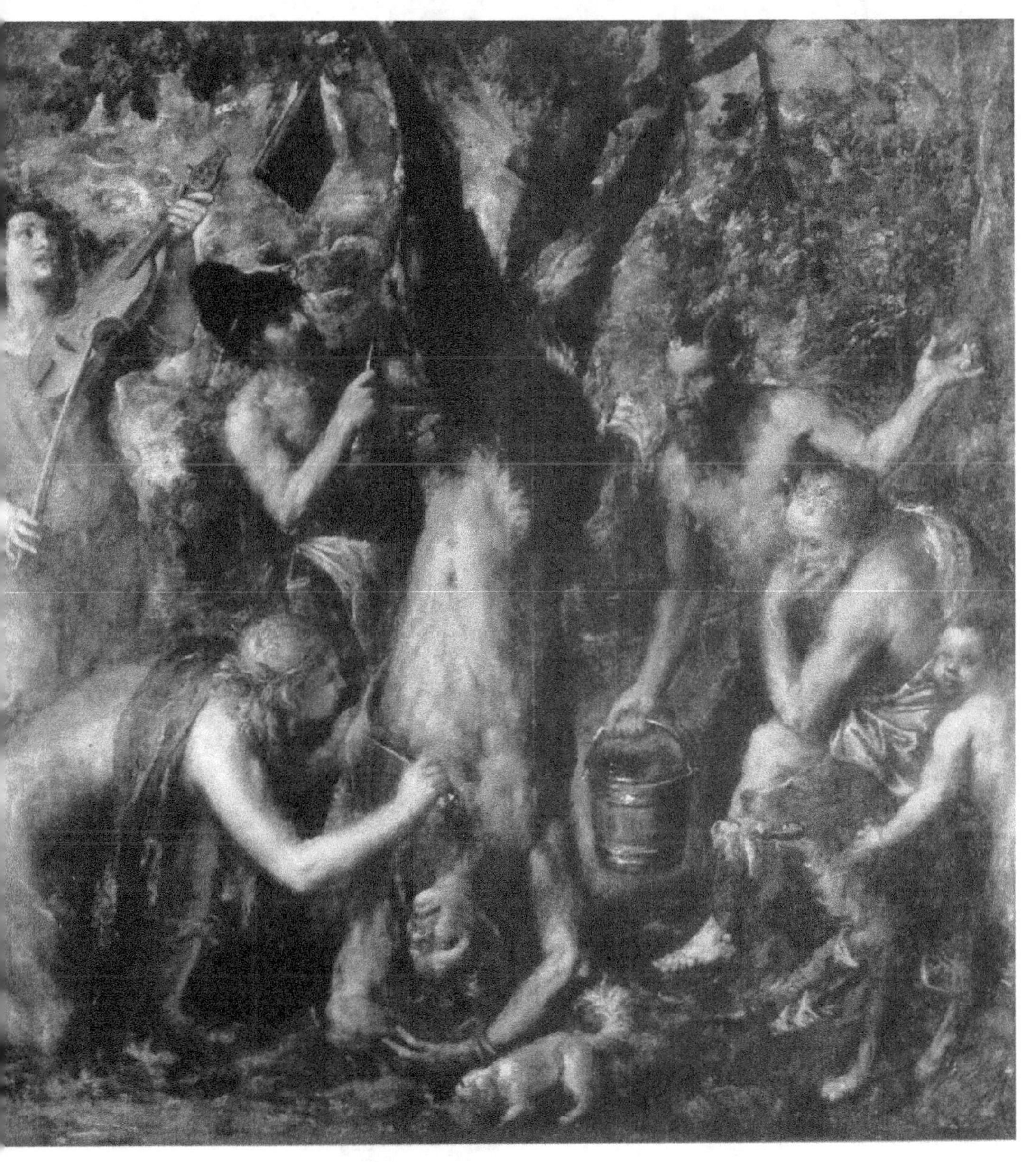

Titian, The Flaying of Marsyas, c. 1570-76, Kromeriz,

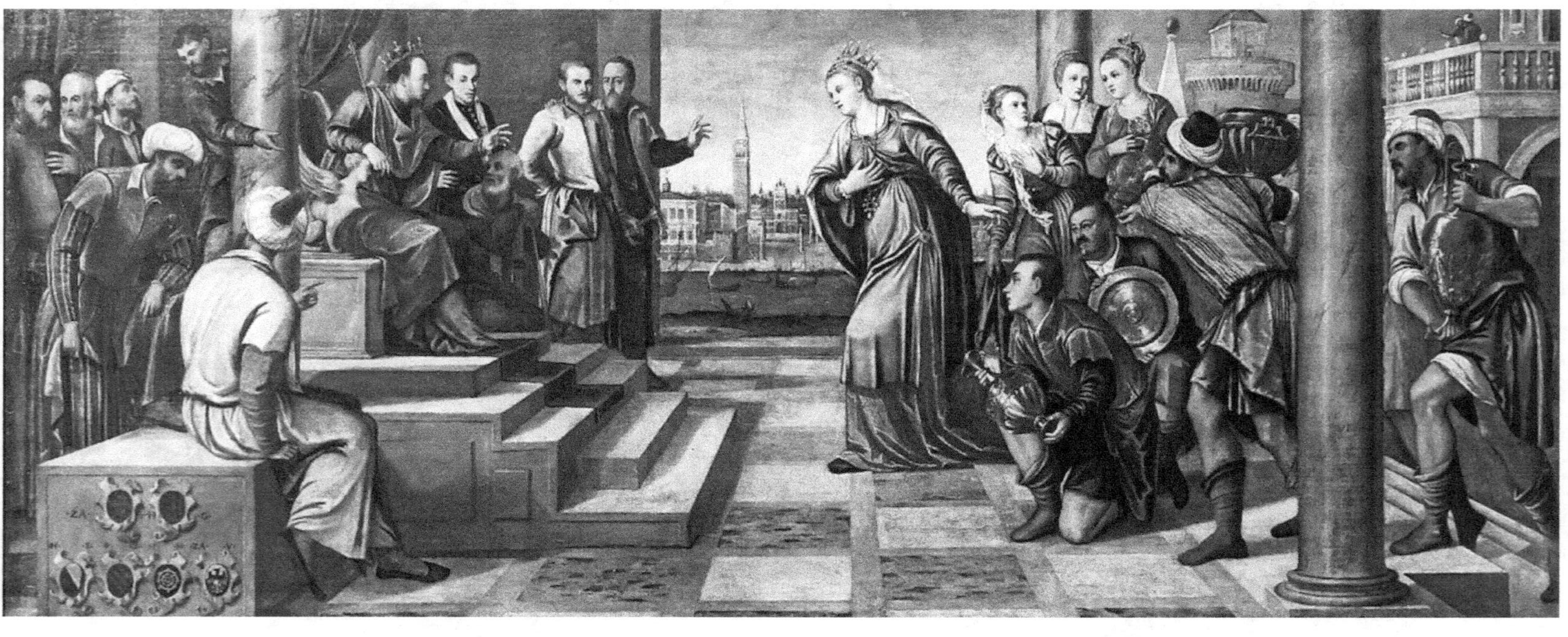

Paolo Veronese, Sacristy, Visit of the Queen of Sheba To Solomon, Venice

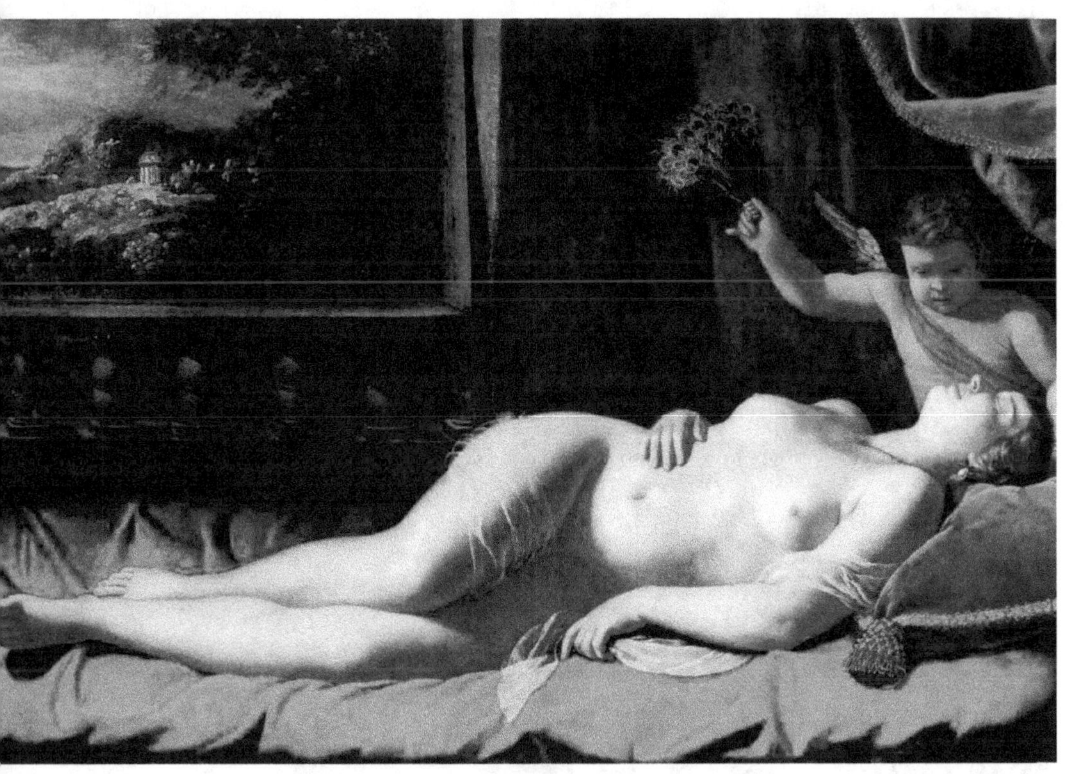

Artemisia Gentileschi, Sleeping Venus, 1625-30,
Barbara Piasecka Johnson Foundation, Princeton, New Jersey

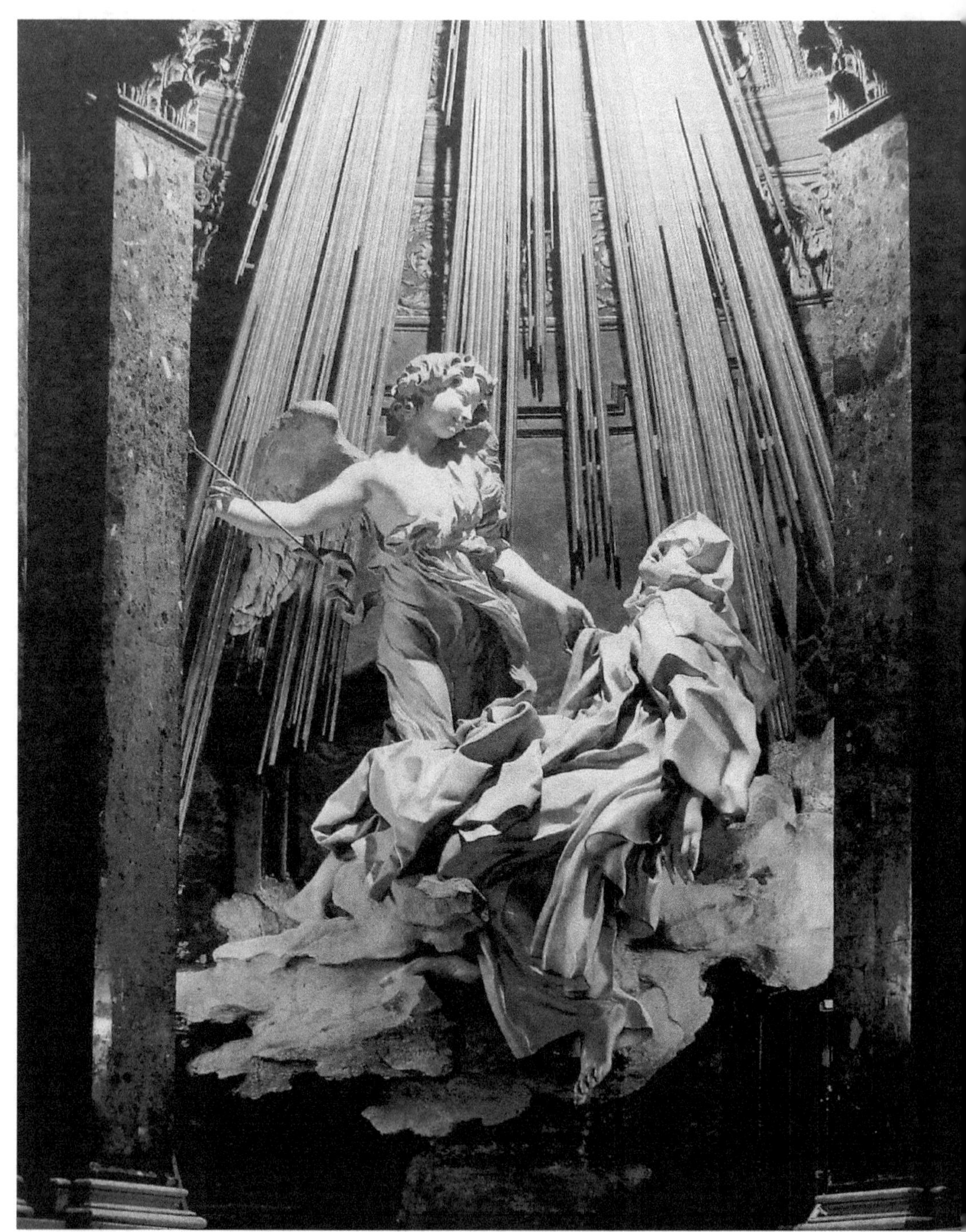

Gianlorenzo Bernini, The Ecstasy of St Theresa, 1652, Rome

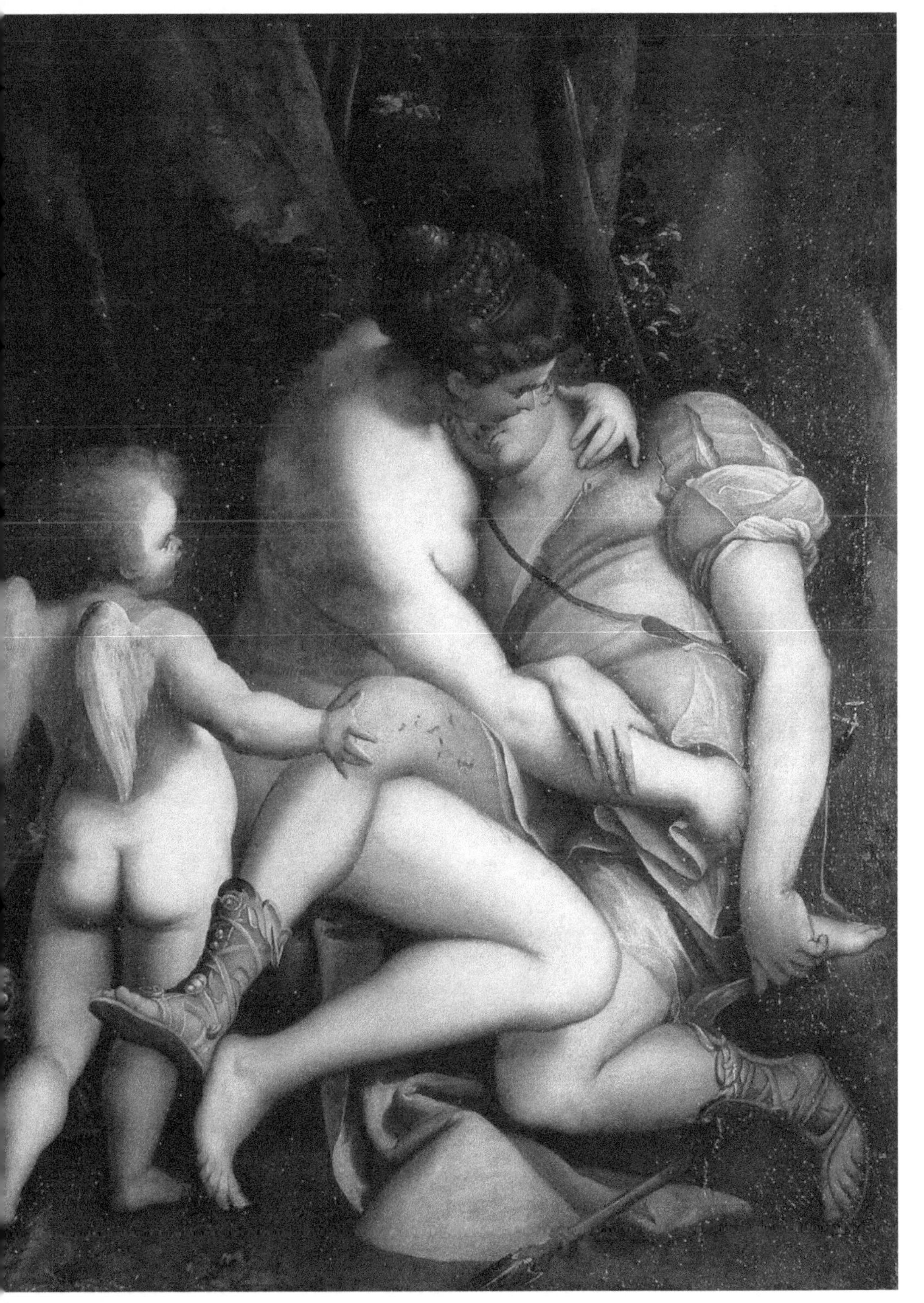

Luca Cambiaso, Venus and Adonis, c. 1565

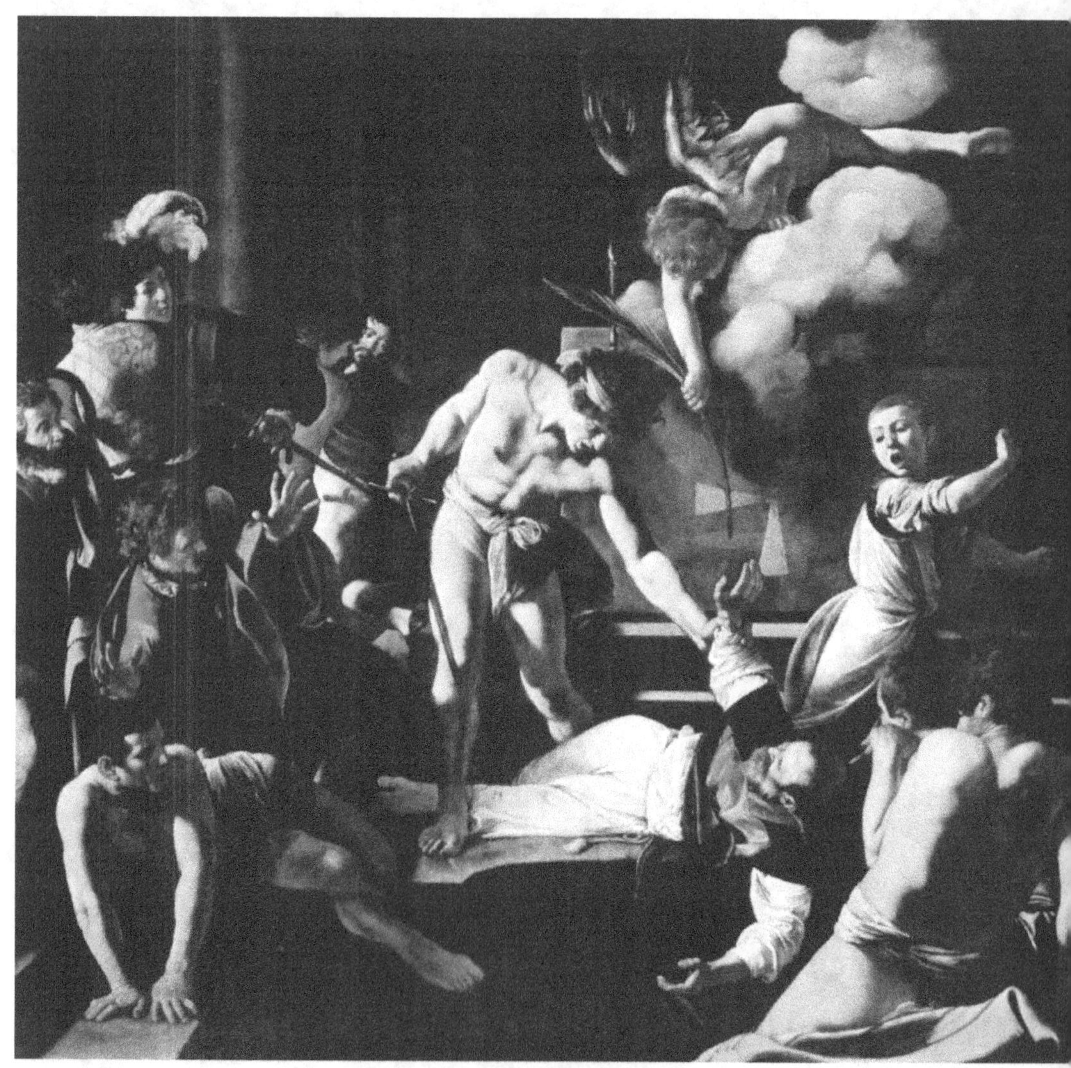

Caravaggio, The Martyrdom of St Matthew, 1600-01,
San Luigi dei Francesci, Rome

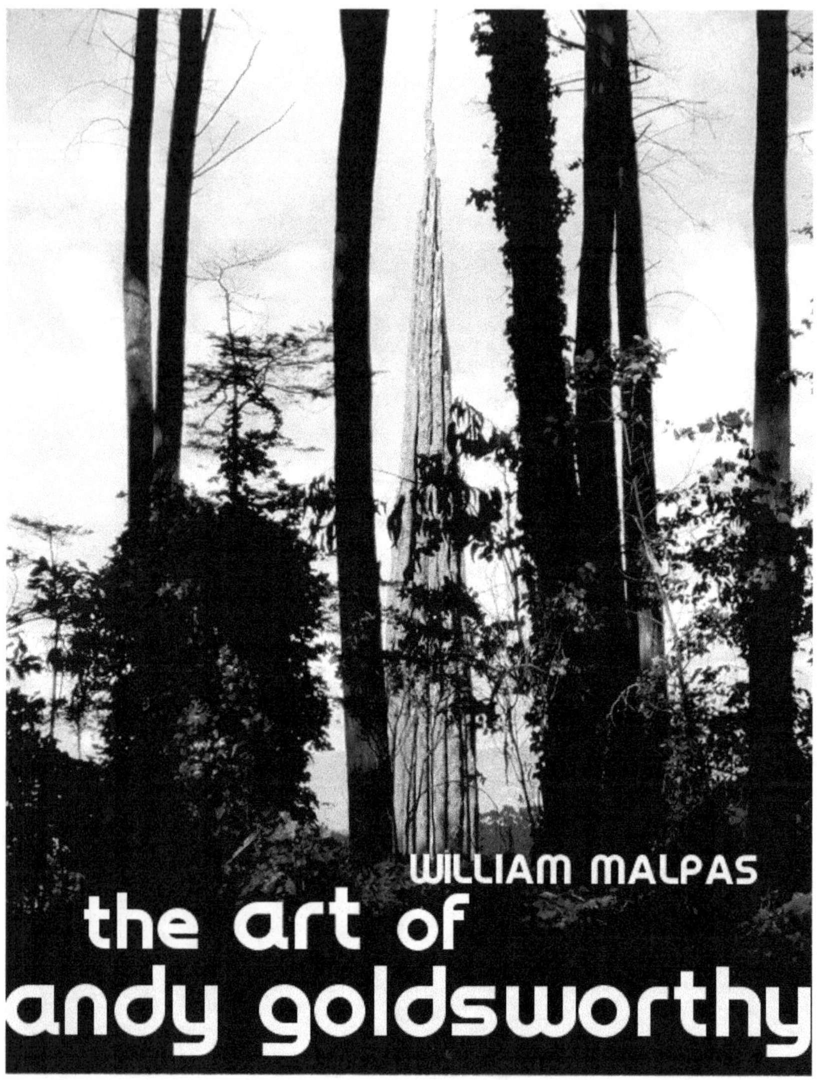

This is the most comprehensive and detailed account of the art of Andy Goldsworthy available.

This study of Andy Goldsworthy discusses all of Goldsworthy's major exhibitions, books and projects, including the *Sheepfolds* project; *Garden of Stones* in New York; TV and dance collaborations; and the books *Wood, Stone, Time* and *Passage.* William Malpas surveys all of Goldsworthy's output, and analyzes his relation with other land artists such as Robert Smithson, the Christos, Walter de Maria, Chris Drury, Richard Long and David Nash; women sculptors; sculpture in the modern era; and Goldsworthy's place in the contemporary British art scene.

The book has been updated and revised for this new edition.

ISBN 9781861714107 Pbk ISBN 9781861714114 Hbk
Fully illustrated www.crmoon.com

MAURICE SENDAK

& the art of children's book illustration

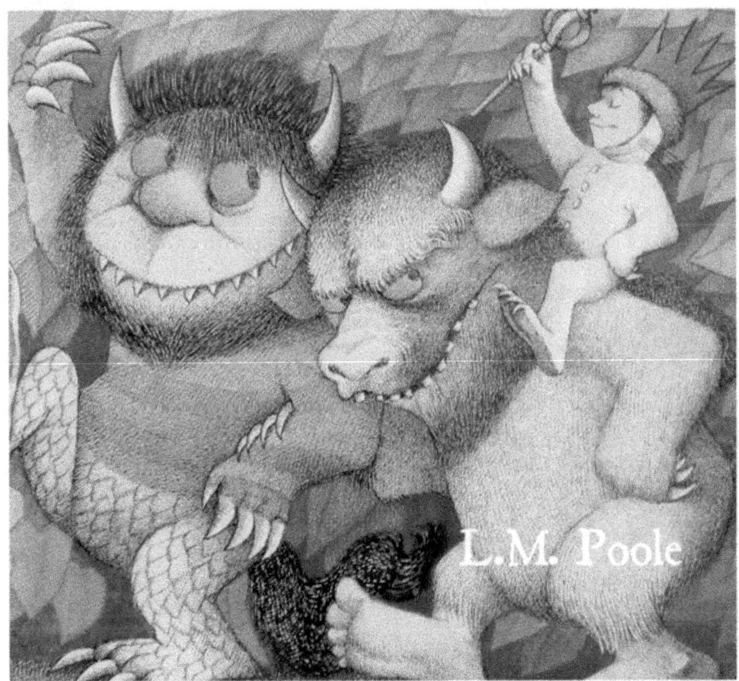

Maurice Sendak is the widely acclaimed American children's book author and illustrator. This critical study focuses on his famous trilogy, *Where the Wild Things Are, In the Night Kitchen* and *Outside Over There*, as well as the early works and Sendak's superb depictions of the Grimm Brothers' fairy tales in *The Juniper Tree*. L.M. Poole begins with a chapter on children's book illustration, in particular the treatment of fairy tales. Sendak's work is situated within the history of children's book illustration, and he is compared with many contemporary authors.

Fully illustrated. The book has been revised and updated for this edition.
ISBN 9781861714282 Pbk ISBN 9781861713469 Hbk

CRESCENT MOON PUBLISHING

web: www.crmoon.com e-mail: cresmopub@yahoo.co.uk

ARTS, PAINTING, SCULPTURE

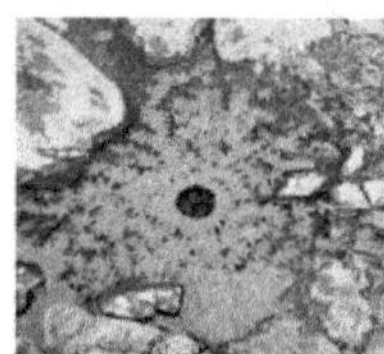

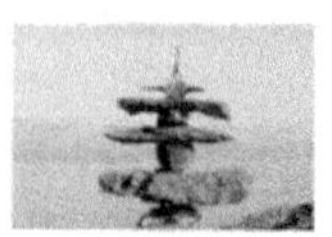

The Art of Andy Goldsworthy
Andy Goldsworthy: Touching Nature
Andy Goldsworthy in Close-Up
Andy Goldsworthy: Pocket Guide

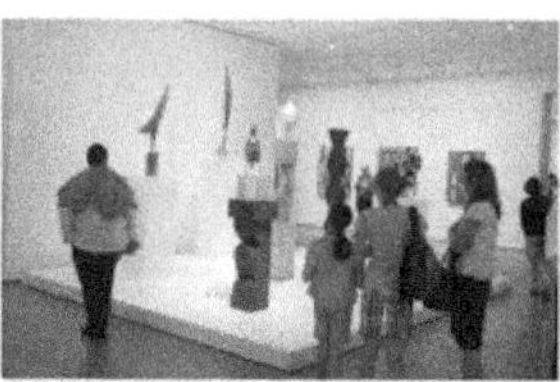

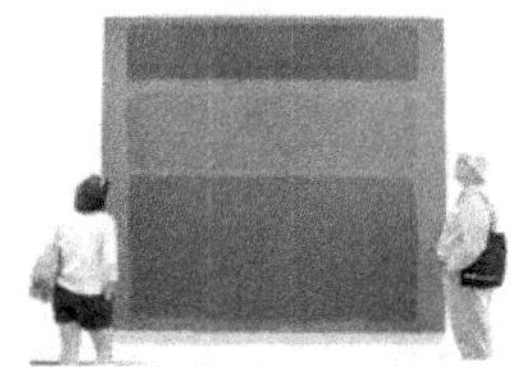

Andy Goldsworthy In America
Land Art: A Complete Guide
The Art of Richard Long
Richard Long: Pocket Guide
Land Art In the UK
Land Art in Close-Up
Land Art In the U.S.A.
Land Art: Pocket Guide
Installation Art in Close-Up

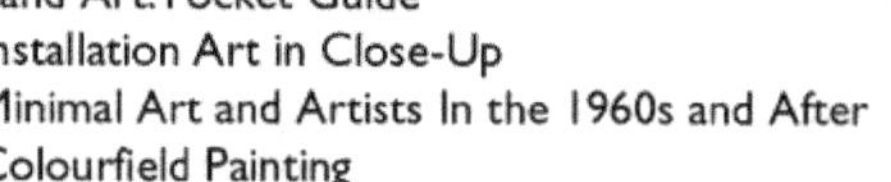

Minimal Art and Artists In the 1960s and After
Colourfield Painting

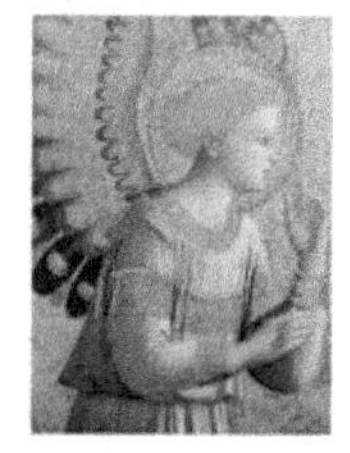

Land Art DVD, TV documentary
Andy Goldsworthy DVD, TV documentary
The Erotic Object: Sexuality in Sculpture From Prehistory to the Present Day
Sex in Art: Pornography and Pleasure in Painting and Sculpture
Postwar Art
Sacred Gardens: The Garden in Myth, Religion and Art
Glorification: Religious Abstraction in Renaissance and 20th Century Art
Early Netherlandish Painting

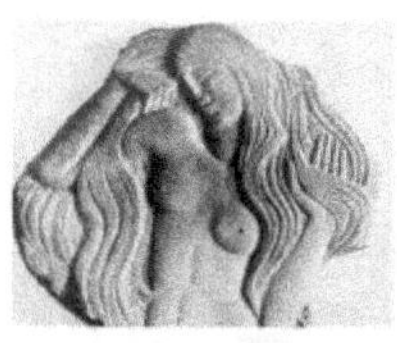

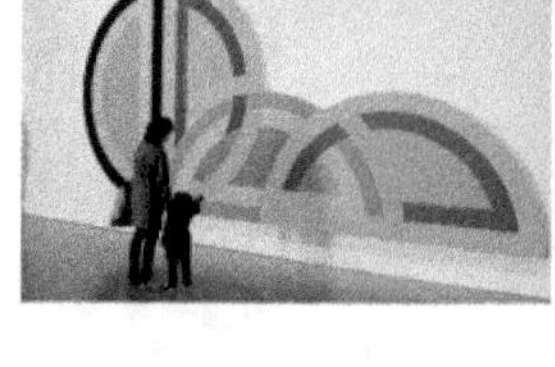

Leonardo da Vinci
Piero della Francesca
Giovanni Bellini
Fra Angelico: Art and Religion in the Renaissance
Mark Rothko: The Art of Transcendence
Frank Stella: American Abstract Artist

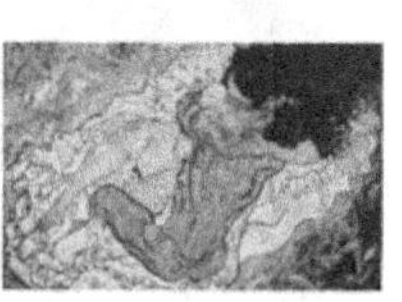

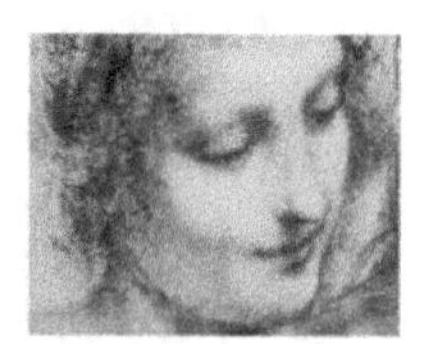

Jasper Johns
Brice Marden
Alison Wilding: The Embrace of Sculpture
Vincent van Gogh: Visionary Landscapes
Eric Gill: Nuptials of God
Constantin Brancusi: Sculpting the Essence of Things
Max Beckmann
Caravaggio
Gustave Moreau

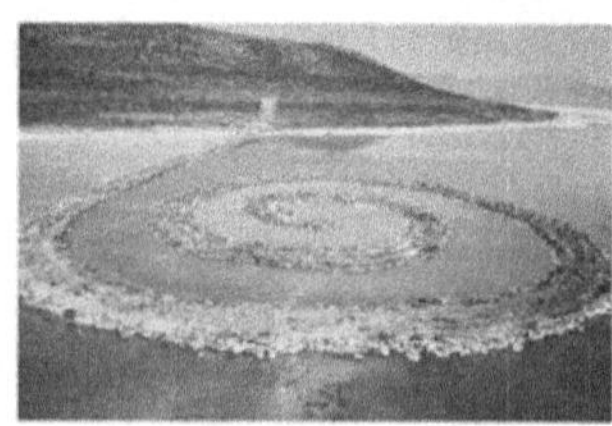

Egon Schiele: Sex and Death In Purple Stockings
Delizioso Fotografico Fervore: Works In Process 1
Sacro Cuore: Works In Process 2
The Light Eternal: J.M.W. Turner
The Madonna Glorified: Karen Arthurs

LITERATURE

J.R.R. Tolkien: The Books, The Films, The Whole Cultural Phenomenon
J.R.R. Tolkien: Pocket Guide
Tolkien's Heroic Quest
The *Earthsea* Books of Ursula Le Guin
Beauties, Beasts and Enchantment: Classic French Fairy Tales
German Popular Stories by the Brothers Grimm
Philip Pullman and *His Dark Materials*
Sexing Hardy: Thomas Hardy and Feminism
Thomas Hardy's *Tess of the d'Urbervilles*
Thomas Hardy's *Jude the Obscure*
Thomas Hardy: The Tragic Novels
Love and Tragedy: Thomas Hardy
The Poetry of Landscape in Hardy
Wessex Revisited: Thomas Hardy and John Cowper Powys
Wolfgang Iser: Essays and Interviews
Petrarch, Dante and the Troubadours
Maurice Sendak and the Art of Children's Book Illustration
Andrea Dworkin
Cixous, Irigaray, Kristeva: The *Jouissance* of French Feminism
Julia Kristeva: Art, Love, Melancholy, Philosophy, Semiotics and Psychoanalysis
Hélene Cixous I Love You: The *Jouissance* of Writing
Luce Irigaray: Lips, Kissing, and the Politics of Sexual Difference
Peter Redgrove: Here Comes the Flood
Peter Redgrove: Sex-Magic-Poetry-Cornwall
Lawrence Durrell: Between Love and Death, East and West
Love, Culture & Poetry: Lawrence Durrell
Cavafy: Anatomy of a Soul
German Romantic Poetry: Goethe, Novalis, Heine, Hölderlin
Feminism and Shakespeare
Shakespeare: Love, Poetry & Magic
The Passion of D.H. Lawrence
D.H. Lawrence: Symbolic Landscapes
D.H. Lawrence: Infinite Sensual Violence
Rimbaud: Arthur Rimbaud and the Magic of Poetry
The Ecstasies of John Cowper Powys
Sensualism and Mythology: The Wessex Novels of John Cowper Powys
Amorous Life: John Cowper Powys and the Manifestation of Affectivity (H.W. Fawkner)
Postmodern Powys: New Essays on John Cowper Powys (Joe Boulter)
Rethinking Powys: Critical Essays on John Cowper Powys
Paul Bowles & Bernardo Bertolucci
Rainer Maria Rilke
Joseph Conrad: *Heart of Darkness*
In the Dim Void: Samuel Beckett
Samuel Beckett Goes into the Silence
André Gide: Fiction and Fervour
Jackie Collins and the Blockbuster Novel
Blinded By Her Light: The Love-Poetry of Robert Graves
The Passion of Colours: Travels In Mediterranean Lands
Poetic Forms

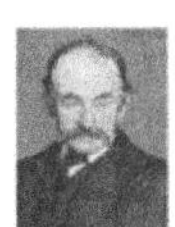
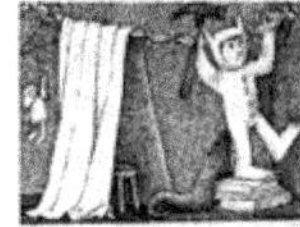
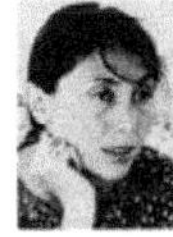
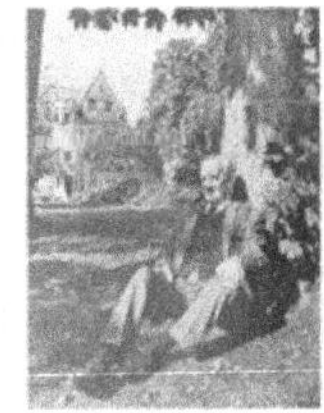
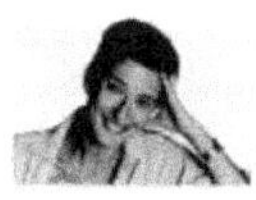
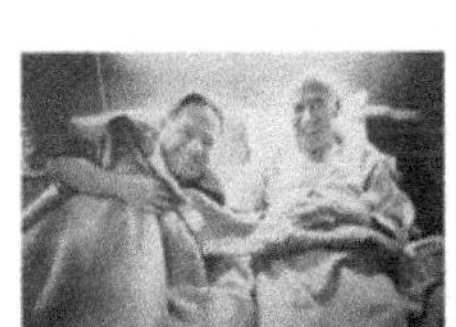
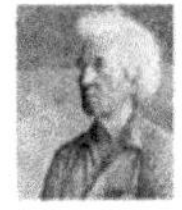
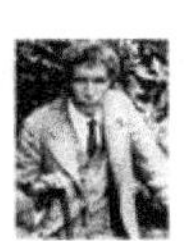
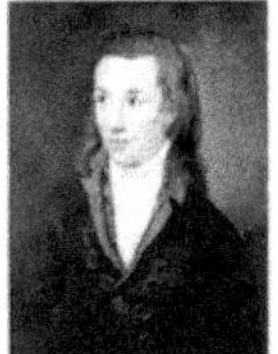

POETRY

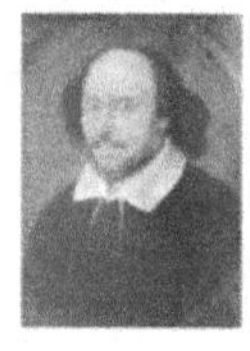
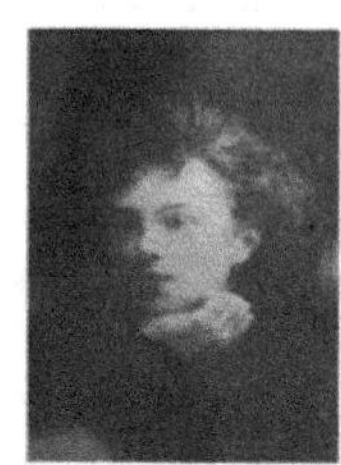

Ursula Le Guin: Walking In Cornwall
Peter Redgrove: Here Comes The Flood
Peter Redgrove: Sex-Magic-Poetry-Cornwall
Dante: Selections From the Vita Nuova
Petrarch, Dante and the Troubadours
William Shakespeare: Sonnets
William Shakespeare: Complete Poems
Blinded By Her Light: The Love-Poetry of Robert Graves
Emily Dickinson: Selected Poems

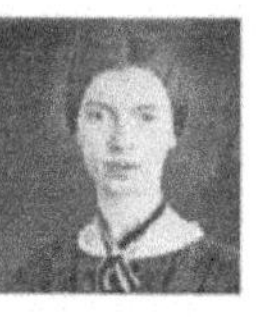

Emily Brontë: Poems
Thomas Hardy: Selected Poems
Percy Bysshe Shelley: Poems
John Keats: Selected Poems
Joh n Keats: Poems of 1820

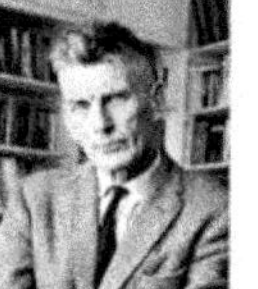
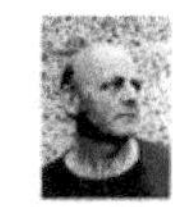

D.H. Lawrence: Selected Poems
Edmund Spenser: Poems
Edmund Spenser: Amoretti
John Donne: Poems

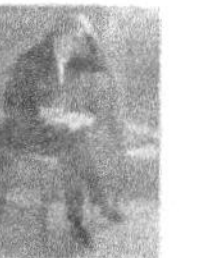
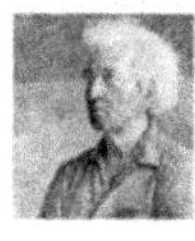

Henry Vaughan: Poems
Sir Thomas Wyatt: Poems
Robert Herrick: Selected Poems

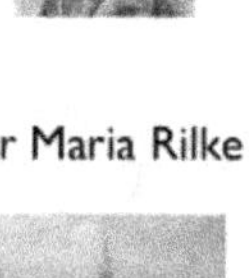

Rilke: Space, Essence and Angels in the Poetry of Rainer Maria Rilke
Rainer Maria Rilke: Selected Poems
Friedrich Hölderlin: Selected Poems
Arseny Tarkovsky: Selected Poems
Arthur Rimbaud: Selected Poems
Arthur Rimbaud: A Season in Hell

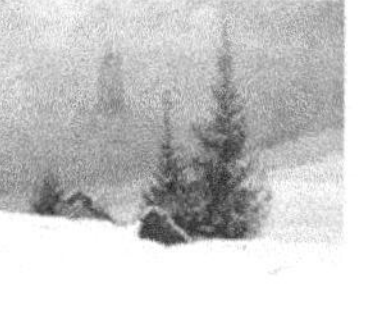

Arthur Rimbaud and the Magic of Poetry
Novalis: Hymns To the Night
German Romantic Poetry
Paul Verlaine: Selected Poems
Elizaethan Sonnet Cycles

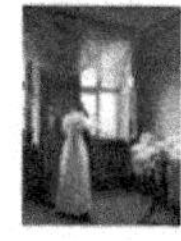
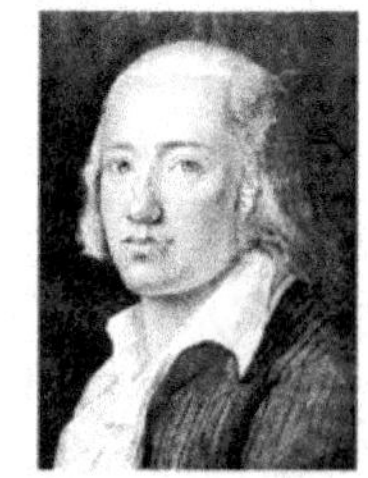
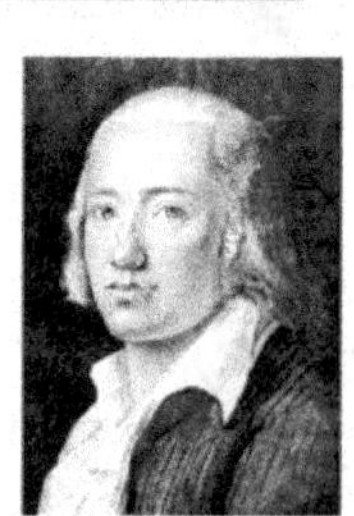

D.J. Enright: By-Blows
Jeremy Reed: Brigitte's Blue Heart
Jeremy Reed: Claudia Schiffer's Red Shoes
Gorgeous Little Orpheus

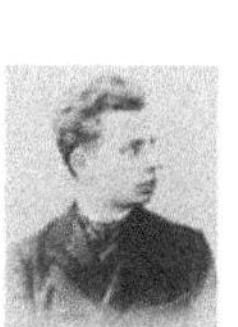

Radiance: New Poems
Crescent Moon Book of Nature Poetry
Crescent Moon Book of Love Poetry
Crescent Moon Book of Mystical Poetry
Crescent Moon Book of Elizabethan Love Poetry
Crescent Moon Book of Metaphysical Poetry
Crescent Moon Book of Romantic Poetry
Pagan America: New American Poetry

MEDIA, CINEMA, FEMINISM and CULTURAL STUDIES

J.R.R. Tolkien: The Books, The Films, The Whole Cultural Phenomenon
J.R.R. Tolkien: Pocket Guide
The *Lord of the Rings* Movies: Pocket Guide
The Cinema of Hayao Miyazaki
Hayao Miyazaki: *Princess Mononoke*: Pocket Movie Guide
Hayao Miyazaki: *Spirited Away*: Pocket Movie Guide
Tim Burton : Hallowe'en For Hollywood
Ken Russell
Ken Russell: *Tommy*: Pocket Movie Guide
The Ghost Dance: The Origins of Religion
The Peyote Cult

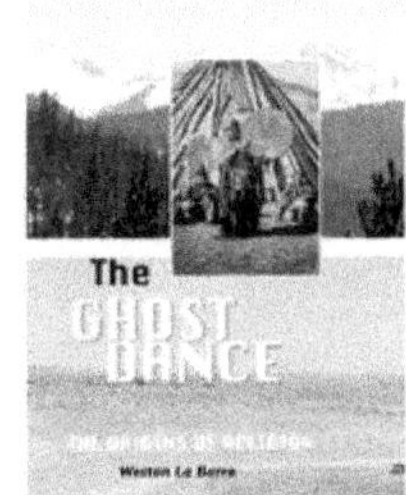

Cixous, Irigaray, Kristeva: The *Jouissance* of French Feminism
Julia Kristeva: Art, Love, Melancholy, Philosophy, Semiotics and Psychoanalysis
Luce Irigaray: Lips, Kissing, and the Politics of Sexual Difference
Hélene Cixous I Love You: The *Jouissance* of Writing
Andrea Dworkin
'Cosmo Woman': The World of Women's Magazines
Women in Pop Music
HomeGround: The Kate Bush Anthology

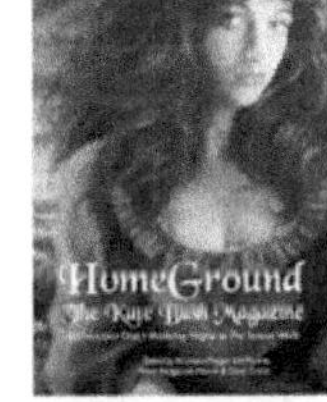

Discovering the Goddess (Geoffrey Ashe)
The Poetry of Cinema
The Sacred Cinema of Andrei Tarkovsky
Andrei Tarkovsky: Pocket Guide
Andrei Tarkovsky: *Mirror*: Pocket Movie Guide
Andrei Tarkovsky: *The Sacrifice*: Pocket Movie Guide
Walerian Borowczyk: Cinema of Erotic Dreams

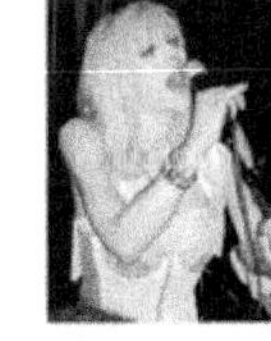

Jean-Luc Godard: The Passion of Cinema
Jean-Luc Godard: *Hail Mary*: Pocket Movie Guide
Jean-Luc Godard: *Contempt*: Pocket Movie Guide
Jean-Luc Godard: *Pierrot le Fou*: Pocket Movie Guide
John Hughes and Eighties Cinema
Ferris Bueller's Day Off: Pocket Movie Guide
Jean-Luc Godard: Pocket Guide

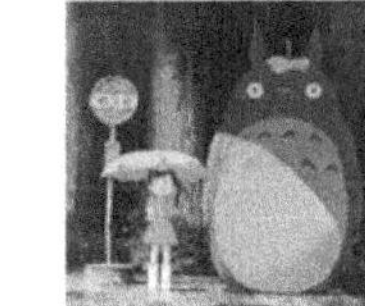

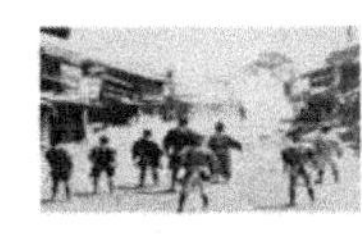

The Cinema of Richard Linklater
Liv Tyler: Star In Ascendance
Blade Runner and the Films of Philip K. Dick
Paul Bowles and Bernardo Bertolucci
Media Hell: Radio, TV and the Press
An Open Letter to the BBC
Detonation Britain: Nuclear War in the UK

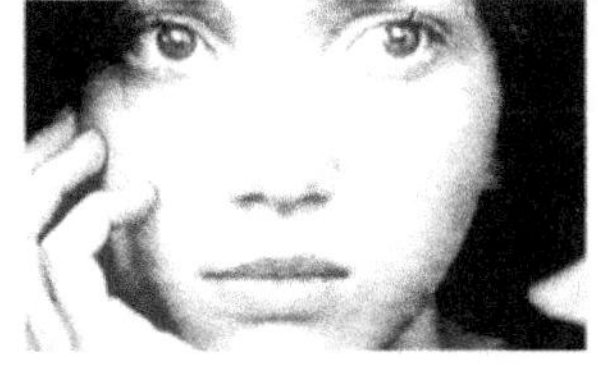

Feminism and Shakespeare
Wild Zones: Pornography, Art and Feminism
Sex in Art: Pornography and Pleasure in Painting and Sculpture
Sexing Hardy: Thomas Hardy and Feminism

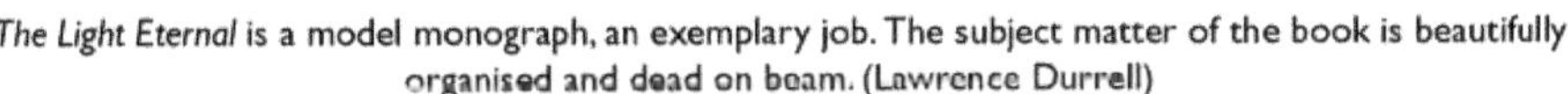

The Light Eternal is a model monograph, an exemplary job. The subject matter of the book is beautifully organised and dead on beam. (Lawrence Durrell)
It is amazing for me to see my work treated with such passion and respect. (Andrea Dworkin)

CRESCENT MOON PUBLISHING
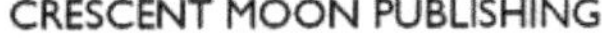
P.O. Box 1312, Maidstone, Kent, ME14 5XU, Great Britain. www.crmoon.com

cresmopub@yahoo.co.uk   www.crescentmoon.org.uk

www.ingramcontent.com/pod-product-compliance
Lightning Source LLC
LaVergne TN
LVHW020513100826
845148LV00003B/769